PLAYING WITH THE

Devil

About the Author

Marcus F. Griffin (Fort Collins, Colorado) is a prolific author and has been a student and teacher of metaphysics and the paranormal for over 29 years. A columnist for the popular website Ghostvillage.com, Griffin has served as a paranormal research consultant on documentary films, broadcast programs, and books. Visit him at MarcusFGriffin.com.

PLAYING WITH THE

Devil

MARCUS F. GRIFFIN

THE TRUE STORY OF A ROCK BAND'S TERRIFYING ENCOUNTERS WITH THE DARK SIDE

Llewellyn Publications
Woodbury, Minnesota

FIRST EDITION
First Printing, 2013

Book design by Donna Burch
Cover art: iStockphoto.com/12867513/-M-I-S-H-A-, 19079686/g_muradin
Cover design by Kevin R. Brown
Editing by Andrea Neff

Llewellyn Publications is a registered trademark of Llewellyn Worldwide Ltd.

Library of Congress Cataloging-in-Publication Data (Pending)
ISBN: 978-0-7387-3688-4

Llewellyn Publications
A Division of Llewellyn Worldwide Ltd.
2143 Wooddale Drive
Woodbury, MN 55125-2989
www.llewellyn.com

Printed in the United States of America

For Charlie, Tony, Steve, and Jeff.
We have touched the other side.

Contents

Note from the Author

Dear reader, the story I am about to tell you is true. However, the names and locations have been changed to protect the innocent from the vagaries of time.

I should also tell you that while I have done my best to give you a clear, accurate, and true account of what I experienced, the majority of the events I will describe to you in this book happened over thirty years ago. Many of the people involved in those events are still alive. Some are not. And of those who remain, few were willing to speak with me about that long-ago time. Even though my memories of the events that follow are vivid and intact, to allow you the most intimate view of these events I will be describing personal encounters and conversations in great detail. To an extent I will, of course, be paraphrasing the actual conversations that took place.

—Marcus

CHRONICLE ONE
The Poem

It was a typical summer day in northern Colorado, dry and hot under a cloudless sky. As I drove along a backcountry road in a 1971 Camaro SS equipped with a set of five-dollar tires, I had no idea that my life was about to change forever. Trice, the bass player for the band I was playing with at the time, was riding in the car with me that day, and as we drove along we were having our usual conversation on topics like music, girls, partying, and other such desires that young men in their early twenties like to talk about.

It was very warm that day, and the heat and the rough gravel eventually took their toll on the Camaro's cheap tires. The inevitable blowout came without warning. After pulling the car off to the side of the road and discovering that the spare was also flat, Trice and I set off on what promised to be a very long walk back to civilization. It was 1980, and we didn't have mobile phones in those days, at least not ones that the average person could afford. And we were just average young men.

It was about ten minutes into our walk that the world started to become surreal to me. Everything started to look different. Everything *felt* different. Suddenly I was hearing a faint buzzing sound. Pretty soon I discovered that I wasn't hearing the buzzing sound with my ears. It was inside my head. Then the trees along the side of the road grabbed my attention. I couldn't keep my eyes or my mind off them. The leaves of the trees seemed to churn and swirl with an energy force that I was somehow not only seeing but also *feeling*. This sensation was, of course, entirely new to me. I'd never had any psychic or mystical experiences. I started to think I was sick, maybe having a heat stroke or something. I asked Trice to sit down with me at the side of the road for a few minutes.

My attention was inexplicably drawn to the leaves in one nearby tree. I don't even remember what kind of tree it was. As I sat there thinking and resting, the sensation of swirling energies overtook me to the point where I couldn't tell the difference between my own self and anything else. I seemed to be lost in space, lost in time. And this was my first experience with lost time, my first experience with the supernatural.

When I finally returned to something approaching ordinary awareness, I wasn't sitting on the side of the road anymore. I was in the basement of the house in which I was living at the time! How could that be? I looked around. I found myself surrounded by the members of the rock 'n' roll band I was playing with at that time. They all had very scared looks on their faces.

Then I noticed that I had a pencil and a piece of paper clenched tightly in my fist. When I unfolded the paper and read what was written on it, it made no sense at all. It looked like two or three poems, very badly written poems, all mishmashed together in some strange, deliberate fashion. I didn't even recognize the handwriting. I held the paper in front of my bandmates. "Who wrote this crap?" I asked. The guys were staring at me like I was crazy, and almost in unison, they raised their eyebrows and said, "You did!"

"Bullshit!" I exclaimed. "Not me!" I went on to explain to them that I was a much better poet than this and that whoever wrote this garbage just sucked. They backed off, at least physically, but then one after another they assured me that not only had I written what was on the paper, but also that for the last half an hour I had been repeating what I had written over and over "like some kind of a chant," the drummer said. One of the other guys added that I had been going on and on about the "gray man" who had been walking with me on the trek back to the house. All four of the guys said that I had explained to them that *he* had told me what to write down on the sheet of paper.

I looked down at my watch. It was 3:33 in the afternoon.

The Ghost in the Machine, Part One

It all began with 3:33. Numbers on a clock. Clear. Simple. Mundane. And yet, in a way that none of us could have possibly known at the time, *elegant*. Elegant, yes, but also *terrifying*. It began with something seemingly powerless, something most people wouldn't have given a second thought: a poem. A poem that in reality was a riddle that, once solved, became a map. A map that led us to an entity far more powerful than any of us could have ever imagined. This entity was the key to attaining everything we had ever desired: fame, money, and power. All the entity asked from us in return was our cooperation. All that was required of us was to do as it commanded.

Yes, this is how it all began. With numbers on a clock. But this is not where our *story* begins. Our story begins the best way possible for five young men living in 1980: with sex, partying, and rock 'n' roll. Does our story start off dramatically, perhaps even sounding a bit exaggerated? *Of course it does*. Our story begins this way because that's the way it began for *us*.

And exactly who, you might be wondering, are *we*? We were the five young men who made up the music group known as Entropy. We're not famous musicians. We never were. Not outside of our home state of Colorado, anyway. And you've probably never even heard the name of the band before now. So if not, dear reader, allow me to tell you our story. Allow me to tell you the story of five talented musicians, our lyrical muse, and the entity that changed our lives forever. A story I call *Playing with the Devil*.

The Genesis of Entropy
1977
3:33—Marcus

As I was entering my senior year in high school, my mother and stepfather moved my sister and me to a nondescript, middle-class subdivision in Fort Collins, Colorado, about thirty or so miles from where we had previously lived in the Rocky Mountains. The house they chose for us was nice enough, a single-story ranch with a large basement that I quickly claimed as my bedroom. I was quite happy with my new space, as I recall. The new school system, however, was a completely different story.

At this school, I was an outsider. A longhair. The only bright side of my new school was the music department, which was enormous, clean, and stocked with top-of-the-line instruments by such epic manufacturers as Selmer and Steinway. The instructors were no sluffs themselves. Many of them were considered some of the top high school music teachers in the country. The school's music department was certainly an inspiring place to be for anyone who could play an instrument, but at that point in my life I was not yet a musician.

That isn't to say I had anything against music. Quite the contrary. In fact, I had been immersed in music from the day I was born. I cannot recall a single day of my youth when I wasn't exposed to some form of music. The first thing my father would do every day upon returning home from work was put a Beatles album on the stereo system. My mother constantly had the radio playing in the house and in the car. I came to love music, even though I couldn't yet play an instrument myself. Sure, I'd had a few brushes with my own musicianship here and there, but nothing really worth bragging about.

When I was seven years old, my parents bought me a secondhand acoustic guitar and even supplied me with lessons at a local music store. But the guitar they had chosen for me was so cheaply made and difficult to play that I quickly became frustrated with the instrument. After constantly complaining about the quality of the guitar to my parents, they refused to purchase a better one until I put a little more effort into working with the one I already had. I spent weeks eyeballing a brand-new 1967 Fender Stratocaster that was hanging on the wall at the music store where I was taking lessons. Even in those days a new Fender Stratocaster was a pricey guitar, and one that in mint condition would be worth a small fortune in today's market. Not that the guitar would have remained in mint condition had I gotten my grubby little seven-year-old hands on it.

Other than my short stint as a prepubescent, wannabe guitar god, the only experiences I'd had with music were in choir classes, which I took religiously throughout high school. I took the classes, yes, but I never really took them seriously, even though more than one of my choir teachers told me I could easily become a top-notch vocalist with a little dedication and a whole lot of work. But back in those days, like most guys my age, I wasn't interested in being dedicated and working hard. Back then I was interested in one thing and one thing only. This was, of course, dating girls. Or to be completely honest with you, having sex with them. And as I discovered soon enough, getting girls to have sex with you was a whole lot easier if you were in a rock 'n' roll band.

5:55—Chuck

I was seventeen years old the day I met Chuck Weber. I had gone into the men's room at my new high school to take a piss, and just as I stepped up to the urinal, Chuck came rushing in and proceeded to beat the shit out of two jocks who had his best friend Bob's head stuffed inside a toilet and were giving him a swirlie.

Chuck had jet-black hair that hung just above his shoulders. He was dressed in a Kiss T-shirt underneath a blue denim jacket. The back of Chuck's jacket was imprinted with a strange word I had never seen before. This word was *Ryad*.

I found out later that day that Ryad (pronounced rye-ad) was the name of Chuck's rock 'n' roll band, although at the time he and Bob were the band's only standing members.

Chuck wasn't a big guy by any means, medium to smallish in stature, and I found myself quite amused and impressed by his bravery. So impressed, in fact, that upon exiting the bathroom, I approached Chuck and told him so. After exchanging greetings and names, I asked Chuck about the strange name on the back of his jacket. With a broad, proud smile, he informed me that he was a guitarist and that the name belonged to the band he was in the process of forming. Upon hearing this, I found myself fascinated by the concept of going to school with someone who played in a rock 'n' roll band. It somehow made the time I spent there more tolerable.

Before long, having conversations with Chuck and Bob became commonplace. We oftentimes would chat about girls and our mutual hatred for school and academics, but our discussions quickly became centered on music. Chuck was a huge fan of the band Kiss, as were a lot of kids in those days, and he even had an Ibanez Iceman to prove it, the very guitar favored by Kiss frontman Paul Stanley.

As it turned out, Chuck lived very close to me, just at the end of my block. One day Chuck invited me to visit him at his home, where he lived with his mother. Chuck's father, I soon discovered, had been killed in action a few years earlier. Chuck was eager to show me his bedroom and his guitar, which, as I previously mentioned, was a glossy, black

Ibanez Iceman with all the dressings. Seeing Chuck's guitar brought up images and memories of the Fender Stratocaster I had so pined for as a kid, and I remember asking him if he wouldn't mind teaching me a few chords if I happened to acquire a guitar of my own one day. Chuck told me he would be delighted to show me what he knew, but also pointed out that he was just learning how to play himself and that his current skills were limited. Well, Chuck's guitar playing sounded pretty damn good to my ears. I was a senior in high school at the time, a full year ahead of Chuck and Bob, and I would be graduating in just a few months' time.

Thanks to my mother, I already had a job set up at a local manufacturer, and as badly as I wanted a guitar of my own, I instead purchased a 1971 Camaro SS for two thousand dollars in cash I had saved up by doing odd jobs throughout my school days. A guy has to get his priorities straight, after all. A teenage boy with no car equals no girlfriend. And besides, I now had a full-time job, and it didn't take me long to save up enough money to purchase an Ibanez guitar and an amplifier of my own. My new guitar wasn't as cool or expensive as Chuck's Iceman, but it played great and was certainly good enough for an amateur such as myself to learn on.

So there I was, a reasonably good-looking young man with a certificate of graduation, a job, a newly acquired girlfriend named Lori (I told you the whole car thing would pay off), a sweet-ass 1971 Camaro SS, my own guitar, and someone kind enough to teach me how to play the damn thing. I was all set and good to go. So what happened next?

Two days before I was to begin taking guitar lessons from Chuck, I accidentally stuck my hand into the spinning blade of a table saw at the factory where I was working. The cut was so bad that I had to be rushed to the hospital. The thumb on my right hand looked as though it had gone through a meat grinder. The wound was so long and deep that it had to be stitched from the tip of my thumb to the palm of my hand. But despite the fresh wound, I was determined to begin learning how to play the guitar right away. I'm sure that at the time I was quite the sight sitting in Chuck's basement with my new guitar propped on my thigh and a guitar pick duct-taped to the enormous bandage on my right thumb, fumbling to learn how to play my first few chords. My hand hurt like hell, but I wasn't about to let the pain and the stitches in my thumb prevent me from learning to play.

According to Chuck, I was making good progress despite my handicap. So much so, in fact, that he suggested that if I put enough time and effort into learning how to play the instrument, he would be happy to have me join his band as a second guitarist. I was delighted by the idea of playing in a band with Chuck and Bob, and I resolved to become the best musician I could be. I spent every minute of my free time practicing the guitar and taking lessons from Chuck. Six months later, I was starting to feel reasonably confident in my musical abilities and began rehearsing with Bob and Chuck on a regular basis. By then we were the best of friends, and we looked to the future with stars in our eyes. And before long, two new friends and musicians came into our lives—friends and musicians that would change everything.

1:11—L.B.

As soon as I started rehearsing with Bob and Chuck, we began actively searching for a key component that our fledgling band had thus far been without: a drummer. The band also didn't have a lead vocalist. After pondering the time I had spent in my high school choir classes and carefully considering the band's situation, I offered to become Ryad's lead vocalist. At the time I remember thinking, *How hard could it be?*

Well, as it turned out, singing lead for a rock 'n' roll band was plenty hard. After my first few attempts at playing guitar as well as singing lead vocals (all cover songs by major musical acts of the day), it became apparent that I had a lot of work to do. But that was okay, I told myself. We *all* had a lot of work to do if we wanted to become professional musicians. And as the old saying goes, practice makes perfect. I clearly recall that we not only enjoyed practicing, we very much looked forward to it. Especially after L.B. joined our little group.

L.B., aka Sean Miller, lived in the same neighborhood as Chuck and I. When I met Sean, he was just a freshman in high school, a full two years behind Chuck and Bob, who were both juniors. Chuck informed us that Sean was a drummer and was interested in joining our group. This was good (even potentially great) news, but in the beginning we were skeptical because of Sean's age.

About a week later, we all showed up at Chuck's house to audition Sean for the band. Everyone was very excited. Well, at least until we laid eyes on Sean's drum set. To say that Sean's drum set was cheaply made would be a grand understatement. In fact, I remember thinking at the time that the only thing the drum set was missing was a portrait of Mickey Mouse painted on the head of the bass drum.

Just looking at Sean's drums increased our skepticism. But once Sean sat down and started to play, our doubts about his skills quickly vanished. This isn't to say that at the time Sean was a great drummer. Quite the contrary. He was, in fact, just learning how to play, and that much was painfully clear to all of us. But within the margins of the beats Sean was laying down, shades of future greatness began to emerge. Sean was going to be one hell of a drummer some day. That much was clear from the start. And as it turned out, it wouldn't take long for Sean to start making his mark as a musician.

Sean introduced exuberance and a heightened sense of professionalism to the band, and by the end of his sophomore year in high school, he had been offered first chair in the music department's drum section, a feat that previously had never been accomplished by anyone younger than a senior. Within a year's time, Sean's skills as a drummer had increased considerably. Inspired by the aggressive way Sean played the drums, the band decided to give him a nickname. This nickname was "the Pound," but thanks to Chuck, Sean's nickname was quickly shortened to "L.B." At that point in our lives, everyone in the band had made great strides as musicians. But sadly, as is oftentimes the case among musicians, problems began to arise—problems that quickly started tearing the band apart.

In less than six months' time, Ryad was history and all of its members had gone their separate ways. Before I knew it, nearly two years had passed since Ryad had disbanded. The four of us had gone on to pursue our individual music careers with different groups, but speaking for myself, none of them compared to Ryad. Sure, a lot of the bands I had played with over the previous few years were made up of some very talented musicians, but at the very core of these bands, something essential was missing. Something I couldn't quite put my finger on. I had often found myself secretly mourning the end of Ryad and the days spent rehearsing in Chuck's basement. I came to realize that musically, things just didn't feel the same. But all that was about to change. Chuck Weber and L.B. would soon enter my musical life for the second time.

On an overcast morning in the winter of 1979, Chuck and L.B. came to visit me at my home and asked if I would be interested in becoming the lead vocalist and second guitarist for a new band they were forming. Without the slightest hesitation, I agreed to join them in their new musical endeavor. This was an exciting time in our young lives. We had an outstanding drummer, a live-wire guitarist, plus a lead vocalist and rhythm guitarist all wrapped up. All we were missing was the right bass player. But finding him (or her) proved to be more difficult than we had anticipated.

4:44—Trice

After weeks of auditioning local bass players, we had yet to find anyone who met our standards and was a good fit for the band. We were quickly becoming frustrated with the search. In a last-ditch effort to find a bass player, Chuck drove to a local music store and tacked a flyer onto the store's bulletin board. The flyer contained our contact information, an overview of the band and its members, and a description of exactly the type of bass player we were looking for.

Approximately two weeks after Chuck posted the flyer, he received a phone call from an area bass player named Trice Fulbright. Later that same day, Chuck informed L.B. and me about the call. He told us that he'd had a lengthy conversation with Trice and that he had a good feeling about him. Chuck seemed confident that Trice was just the kind of bass player we had been searching for, "just as long as his fingers can back up his bullshit," Chuck had told us, half-jokingly.

As it turned out, Trice's fingers were more than up for the challenge. Chuck felt that it would be a good idea to meet Trice in person and listen to him play before inviting him to audition for the band. L.B. and I both agreed, so Chuck contacted Trice to set up a time and place to meet. We were to meet Trice in Boulder, Colorado, at the house he was living in at the time. L.B. wasn't available to accompany us that day, so Chuck and I headed out to meet Trice on our own.

Upon arriving at Trice's place and exiting the vehicle, we could hear the sound of a bass guitar lofting through the house's open windows. Judging by what we could hear from outside, the playing was excellent. We stepped up and onto the porch and saw that the front door was wide open. Looking inside, we caught our first glimpse of Trice.

From our point of view, Trice appeared to be quite thin and a little shorter than average height. He had sandy, shoulder-length hair and a scraggly goatee. Trice was a very good-looking young man, but the bass guitar he was playing looked even better. Trice was standing in front of an Ampeg amplifier hooked up to a 4 x 12 cabinet. Strapped across his shoulders was a Rickenbacker 4001 stereo bass guitar in all its glory. The guitar had a glossy, clear-coat finish, revealing the natural blonde wood underneath.

But as beautiful as the Rickenbacker was to our eyes, what Trice was playing on it was even more beautiful to our ears. Trice was jamming out "Overture," the opening instrumental from the 1976 album *2112* (pronounced "twenty-one twelve") by the Canadian rock group Rush. And in musician's lingo, he was tearing it up! If you're a

Rush fan or are familiar with this awesome trio, then you already know that replicating their music, the bass lines in particular, is no small feat.

At the time (and to this very day), Rush was one of my all-time favorite rock bands, and I was in awe of the skill and precision with which Trice was performing their music. Not wanting to disturb his playing, Chuck and I just stood there on the porch listening and smiling to each other and to ourselves. Eventually Trice noticed us standing on his porch. He unstrapped his bass, set the instrument in its stand, then came to the door and welcomed us inside.

After having a lengthy and enjoyable conversation with Trice and listening to him play a few more tunes, Chuck and I did everything short of offering him the position with the band on the spot. But we dared not go that far without first setting up a proper audition and consulting with L.B. We informed Trice of our intentions and told him to expect a phone call from us within the next few days. Trice said he would be delighted to come up to Fort Collins for an audition and that he looked forward to hearing back from us.

Filled with satisfaction that we had finally found the right bass player for the band, Chuck and I made the hour-long drive back home.

2:22—Jeff

After our original group, Ryad, disbanded, Chuck had become close friends with Jeff Halloran. Jeff was short and stocky and came across as being quite gruff to people who didn't know him. But once a person won Jeff over and cracked his granite-like exterior, he was a pleasure to hang out with. Jeff would do just about anything to please and protect his friends and loved ones, and the two of us quickly developed an unbreakable bond.

Although Jeff wasn't musically inclined and couldn't play an instrument, he was a brilliant lyricist. He also did anything and everything he could to help out the band. Jeff was our head roadie and resident bodyguard. He made sure we always had plenty of extra guitar strings and drumsticks on hand in case any of them got broken. He saw to it that Chuck was supplied with his obligatory bottle of Jack Daniel's, and that the rest of us had plenty of beer, weed, and munchies on hand in case we were in the mood to do a little partying. We "felt the need" quite often, as I recall. Jeff also made sure that nearly every young lady in town was aware of the band's existence and that our door was always open if any of them cared to stop by for a visit and listen to us play. Happily for us, quite a few of those young ladies took Jeff up on his offer on a regular basis.

And, of course, as I mentioned previously, Jeff was a brilliant lyricist and had already penned more than a few pages of lyrics for the band. One of the songs that Jeff had penned for us (a song that would soon become one of my personal all-time favorites) was about to be played for the very first time by a full band.

In the early spring of 1980, Trice showed up at my house in Fort Collins to audition for the band. Our practice area was in the basement of my home, and the house itself had at one time belonged to my grandparents. My basement was large and rectangular, with a wall separating the stairwell, laundry room, and furnace from the main room. On each end of this wall there were doorways leading to and from the two sections of the basement. Positioned along the wall in the main room were two couches facing the area of the basement where we had our musical equipment set up for rehearsing. At the far end of the room near the stairwell was a large, stone fireplace that had been hand-laid by my grandfather. Exactly why I have described the layout of the basement to you in such detail will become apparent soon enough.

After meeting Trice at the front door and helping him muscle his musical equipment into the basement, we introduced him to Jeff and L.B., both of whom took to Trice as quickly as Chuck and I had. The five of us spent a good hour and a half chatting about music before we got around to playing some of it. We discovered that, similar to the rest of us, Trice had been inspired to learn how to play music by major musical acts of the day, including Kiss, Led Zeppelin, Pink Floyd, and Rush.

Trice, Chuck, and I eventually found our way in front of our amps and behind our guitars, and L.B. positioned himself behind his drum set. We spent the first hour or so of the audition in an impromptu jam session, getting a feel for what it was like to play together. It felt great, and before long Chuck was showing Trice the progressions and chord patterns for a song he and Jeff had written for the band. The song was called "Tamin' the Wood." Chuck had written the music to this song, and Jeff had written the lyrics.

Jeff's lyrics for "Tamin' the Wood" ingeniously integrated a simile of how a band is like a tree. Similar to a tree, a band must have strong roots to become great. It must be provided with plenty of nourishment to thrive. It must be strong yet able to bend without breaking. Jeff's lyrics described how rock 'n' roll fans are like the leaves of a tree. It described how the leaves and the adoration of an audience are the fruit of many years of dedication and hard work.

Trice learned this new song quickly, and after playing it a few times, we had the music and vocals down tight. This alone was evidence enough that the five of us belonged together. We offered Trice the position of bass player, and he accepted without hesitation. At long last, we had a bass player who exceeded our expectations. At long last, our little band was complete. All we needed now was a name.

12:34

July 1980

A little over three months had passed since Trice had joined us, and we still hadn't come up with a name for the band. We were quickly becoming discouraged with the process. But that was about to change. In fact, *everything* was about to change.

One night after the five of us had gathered at my home to rehearse some new music, Chuck and I sat relaxing on one of the couches in the basement. Trice and L.B. had gone home for the evening, and Jeff was sprawled on the floor next to us, lightly napping. As we sat there on the couch, Chuck once again brought up the topic of naming the band. *Not again*, I remember thinking at the time. No matter what name any of us had come up with—and we had come up with quite a few—the five of us seemed forever locked in disagreement. The one thing we all did agree on, however, was that the band's name needed to exude power and strength. The name had to be all-encompassing and define the style of music we played in a single word. As I sat silently musing over the names that had been suggested so far, Chuck spoke aloud a single word. This word was "universe."

"Universe?" I said, repeating the word.

"Yes," Chuck replied, "universe." I immediately understood where Chuck was going with this. The band wanted a name that was big and powerful, and the universe exemplified those themes perfectly. There was, however, one small problem with the name Chuck had come up with for the band: I hated it. And apparently, so did Jeff.

From his resting place on the floor, Jeff groaned and rolled over to face us. He looked up at Chuck and said, "That sucks." He shook his head and added, "You can do better than that." It was at that moment that a word popped into my head. It was a word I had learned in my high school science class. The word was the perfect name for the band, and I was about to speak it aloud to Chuck and Jeff for the very first time.

Before I go any further, I need you to remember the very beginning of this book where I described to you the day that Trice and I had become stranded alongside the road and had made the long walk back home. I described to you my experience with lost time. I described the poem I had written and the "gray man" that had told me what to write down on the sheet of paper. I described how the other members of the band were concerned for my wellbeing. But what I didn't tell you is that, at the time, my bandmates all thought that I had pretty much lost my mind. Hell, there were moments when even *I* thought I was losing my mind. There was no "gray man," I had told myself after the incident. There never was. It was impossible. Things like that just didn't happen. Everyone, including me, thought the concept of a gray man that only I could hear and see was ludicrous. But all that was about to change.

Still sitting next to me on the couch, Chuck shifted uncomfortably. He was perturbed by the bashing Jeff had given the name he had come up with for the band. That much was clear to see. Chuck's brow was furrowed. The basement was illuminated by the flickering light from a single candle, making the lines in his forehead appear exaggerated. Jeff and Chuck sat in silence, glaring at each other. In an effort to break the tension, I spoke aloud the word that had been floating around in my mind for the last few minutes. "Entropy," I said.

"What did you say?" Chuck asked, turning to face me. "Did you say 'entropy'?"

"Yes," I said. "Entropy. If you want a big name for the band, well, there you go. Sure, the universe is big and powerful, but entropy is even more powerful because eventually it's going to kill the universe."

What little I knew about entropy I had learned a few years earlier, and my memory of the subject was vague at best. I was pretty sure that entropy had something to do with linear time. I also recalled that one of my science teachers had taught me that entropy would eventually cause the universe to undergo a sort of "heat death," but I couldn't remember the exact details of that theory.

Chuck raised his arms. He interlocked his fingers behind his head and leaned back on the couch. Jeff gave me a nod and a smile. It was apparent that Chuck and Jeff really liked the new name I had come up with for the band.

"Entropy," Chuck whispered, smiling to himself. Jeff rolled over and lay back down on the floor. I felt satisfied and pleasantly euphoric. I gazed deeply into the shadowy corner at the far end of the basement. I felt the sensation of my conscious mind floating away from me. I started to feel just like I had on the day that Trice and I had the flat tire. I could hear a faint buzzing sound. I was no longer aware of the passing of time or the world around me. I had no idea how long I'd been sitting there on the couch, bathed in flickering candlelight and staring into the corner of the room.

The next thing I remember was feeling incredible pain shooting through my right arm. The pain snapped me out of my trance and back to reality. Cringing, I looked down at my arm and saw that Chuck's left hand was grasped tightly around the meat of my bicep. His fingertips were dug deep into the bare flesh on my arm. It hurt like hell. I was about to ask Chuck exactly what he thought he was doing, but when I looked up and saw his face, my breath seized in my chest and my skin went cold.

Chuck was backed tightly against the corner of the room where the couch met the wall. His face was ghostly white. Tears were streaming from his red eyes. The hair on his arms and head was standing straight up, and a madman's grin crossed his face. Chuck's chest was heaving irregularly, and the breath escaping his lungs sounded more like laughter than breathing. I was as confused as I was frightened by what I was witnessing. I had never seen anything like this before.

Through my fear, I noticed that Chuck was staring at the center of the room. I turned my head and looked in the same direction. At first, what I was seeing was muddled and vague, like the last fading remnants of a dream. Then everything came into focus, and I thought I might be hallucinating. But what I was seeing couldn't possibly have been a hallucination. I was completely sober. My body invol-untarily jerked backward. I tried without success to com-prehend what I was seeing. I was too terrified to move, let alone think.

Hovering in the center of the basement was a gray, face-less apparition in the shape of a man. The apparition raised its arms and gestured toward us. The gesture was exagger-ated, reminiscent of a stage performer bowing to his audi-ence. I tried to scream, but my voice was useless. I wanted to run, but all the strength in my legs had drained away. The entire room started to flux and flicker as if an old black-and-white movie was being projected onto the walls.

Out of the corners of my eyes I was catching glimpses of things even darker than the shadows shuffling around in the corners of the room. Jeff sat up on the floor from where he was resting. He glanced up at me, then looked around the room. Jeff's eyes came to rest on the appari-tion. He shot up from off the floor and screamed, "What the fuck is that?!" The apparition turned its head in Jeff's direction as if to look at him, but the faceless man had no eyes. Jeff stumbled backward and slammed hard against the wall.

As I watched in horror, the apparition rose even higher into the air. A large ring of blue fire formed on the floor at the apparition's feet. The room filled with the sound of crackling static electricity. I could feel the crisp sting of an electrical charge dancing across my skin. I heard a loud whoosh, and the apparition was sucked down into the ring of blue fire, vanishing into nothingness and taking most of the heat and oxygen in the room along with it. The candle had been extinguished, and the room was plunged into darkness. The basement was a vacuum. The air was freezing cold.

I jumped to my feet, gasping for breath. I ran my hand along the wall behind me searching for the light switch and somehow found it on the first try. I flicked the switch, and the basement flooded with light. Chuck was still on the couch and backed tightly into the corner, gasping to catch his breath. I grabbed him by the arm and pulled him up and off the couch. With Jeff in the lead, we rushed into the furnace room and up the stairs. On our way out of the basement, the alarm clock sitting on the fireplace mantle caught my attention. It was exactly 11:11 PM.

Chuck and Jeff stayed over at my house that night, not because they particularly wanted to, but because I had asked them to. As much as it shames me to admit it, I was scared shitless by what we had just experienced in the basement and I didn't want to be alone in the house. In truth, I wouldn't feel comfortable being alone in my own home until many years later.

That night, the three of us stayed awake into the wee hours marveling at what we had experienced. Chuck, who had seen the apparition first and for longer than Jeff and I, was the first to speak about it. He told us that as terrified as he had initially been by the apparition of the gray man, his fear of it had been short-lived. As ridiculous as it sounded, Chuck told us that for him, looking at the gray man had been like watching a talk show host on TV. "Like watching Johnny Carson," he had told us. A supernatural entity had just materialized in my basement, and yet astonishingly, Chuck seemed to be perfectly okay with that. Chuck claimed that he had sensed no threat whatsoever from the gray man. He said that he had felt extreme exhilaration and a touch of anxiety, but no danger of any kind.

Chuck believed that the reason the gray man had appeared in the basement was to deliver a message to us. In Chuck's own words, that message was, "Everything is going to be okay." He believed that the gray man had come to congratulate us on a job well done. He believed that the job well done was choosing the name Entropy for the band. Jeff, on the other hand, wasn't nearly as enthusiastic about the gray man as Chuck was. Jeff pointed out that the gray man hadn't "come" at all, but had "pretty much materialized out of fucking thin air. Shit like that doesn't just happen," he pointed out to Chuck.

For my part, what I had seen in the basement that night changed everything. The apparition and what it implied started chipping away at my beliefs. I had never been a particularly religious man, but now I found myself in the unfamiliar situation of having to consider broader possibilities—possibilities that weren't limited to classic definitions of good and evil. *Was the gray man a ghost?* I wondered. *A demon? An angel? Was he an otherworldly intelligence that my human mind was incapable of comprehending?*

Before that night, I had never seriously considered the possibility of supernatural forces and otherworldly entities, let alone forces and an entity that, for unknown reasons, had manifested in the basement of my house. For me, the experience had been terrifying. And perhaps strangely enough, the part of the encounter that had gotten under my skin the most was the ring of blue fire that had appeared on the ground at the gray man's feet. At least "a ring of blue fire" is the easiest way for me to describe what I had seen. But I couldn't shake the feeling that if I had been able to touch that ring of fire, it wouldn't have felt hot, but ice cold. Not a single one of us was capable of comprehending what that ring of fire was made of. None of us could say with any certainty what the gray man really was or what it wanted from us. None of us had ever experienced the supernatural before, at least not to this extent, and the bottom line was that as far as the paranormal was concerned, we were sailing directly into uncharted waters.

If Chuck was right about the gray man materializing in the basement to congratulate us, then there had to be a connection between us and the entity that we just weren't seeing. *If not*, I asked myself, *why would an entity from another world bother appearing to us in the first place?* There had to be a larger force at work than just a ghostly apparition that liked to emulate talk show hosts. There had to be a good reason why an otherworldly entity that had exhibited tremendous power would bother making contact with the members of a rock 'n' roll band.

Later that same night, Chuck and Jeff asked me if I'd ever experienced any unexplainable phenomena in the house before. They wanted to know if the house itself had any previous history of paranormal activity. To my knowledge, the answer to that question was no. The house had at one time belonged to my grandparents. I had spent nearly every weekend of my youth in the house, and I knew it every bit as well as I did my own self. I had never experienced anything in the house before that had even bordered on being paranormal, nor could I recall anyone in my family experiencing anything unexplainable in the house.

The three of us sat talking for a while longer, but by then it was getting very late. As much as I wanted to continue our conversation, I was mentally and physically exhausted. So were Chuck and Jeff. With more questions than answers spinning inside our heads, we bid each other good night and headed off to sleep.

In the weeks to come, I spent a great deal of time researching the history of my house and interviewing members of my family in an effort to discover if they had any knowledge of deaths or strange happenings that had previously occurred there. I wanted to find out if there was any possible connection between my house's history and the apparition we had witnessed in the basement.

During my research, I discovered that at one time the land my house was built on was an asparagus and peanut farm and that the foundation of the house had supported a barn. I found out that the house itself was nearly one hundred years old and that a single family had owned the property previous to my grandparents purchasing it in the early 1900s. I was unable to find any record of someone dying at my address, and no one in my family could recall a single unexplainable incident taking place on the property. If there was a connection between the apparition in the basement and any former occupants, it would forever remain a mystery.

The next morning, Chuck called Trice and L.B. and told them that we needed to speak with the two of them urgently. They both came over to my house right away. Once Trice and L.B. arrived, Chuck proudly announced that, dependent on everyone's approval, the band finally had a name. Upon hearing the new name, Trice and L.B. enthusiastically gave us the thumbs-up. Everyone in the band was excited about the name Entropy. It was only after explaining to Trice and L.B. what the rest of us had gone through to *get* the name that the atmosphere inside my house changed dramatically.

After listening carefully to Chuck tell the story of what he, Jeff, and I had experienced in the basement the night before, Trice and L.B. developed two very different opinions on the subject. It was obvious by Trice's demeanor that he sincerely believed every word that Chuck had spoken.

But Trice had been raised in a Christian household, and even though his spiritual beliefs had relaxed over the years, it was plain to see that he was confused and concerned by the religious implications of the gray man.

L.B., on the other hand, thought the four of us were completely full of shit, and he wasn't afraid to say so to our faces. He even halfheartedly suggested that the three of us must have been under the influence of heavy-duty narcotics the night before and that the apparition of the gray man had been nothing more than a hallucination.

But L.B. was wrong. That night, none of us had been under the influence of alcohol or drugs of any kind. Sure, everyone in the band (L.B. included) occasionally enjoyed having a few drinks and smoking a little weed, but we hadn't ingested anything that would have caused us to hallucinate. The five of us had zero tolerance for anything that would interfere with our music, and the band had a strict, hands-off policy when it came to hard drugs. But even though we eventually convinced L.B. that we hadn't been under the influence, he brushed off the entire gray man incident as the byproduct of eccentricities and overactive imaginations. But L.B. wouldn't remain a disbeliever for long.

CHRONICLE TWO
The Impossible Man

The Room of Lost Dreams, Part One
October 1980

Over three months had passed since we had witnessed the apparition in the basement, and during that time not a single one of us had experienced anything else out of the ordinary. The gray man soon became little more than a distant memory, and the band was back to business as usual.

We were rehearsing three nights a week by then, and the band's music, the music of Entropy, was tighter than ever. To our ears, the sounds we were laying down were nothing short of impressive. L.B. played his drums with a precision and ferocity that would have made even the God of Thunder proud. Trice's bass lines were every bit as precise, and his playing was becoming more and more technical and progressive all the time. Together, Trice and L.B. made one hell of a fine rhythm section. They had become the nucleus of the band. Chuck's guitar playing was as hot and raw as a live wire. The riffs and chord patterns he had written for our songs were both original and memorable. In contrast to Chuck, my own guitar playing was clean and meticulous. Though I had struggled in earlier years to reproduce the vocals of other singers, in Entropy I excelled. I was also beginning to experiment with synthesizers and sound effects.

The sound Entropy developed was hard for even us to pin down, but I would liken it to a cross between Led Zeppelin and Pink Floyd. Our music was heavy, without question, but with decidedly ethereal overtones. Together we had written and perfected nothing less than a full album's worth of original material. The five of us were very proud of our music and what we had accomplished. We started making noise about producing professional recordings of our music and even setting up live performances. Everything we had ever done musically had led us to this point in our lives. Everything was proceeding as planned. Life was back to normal in our world. Well, at least things were normal until L.B. spent his first night in my guest bedroom upstairs.

With a full set of solid, original material under our belts, we decided it was time to put together a combo house party/ dress rehearsal so we could get used to playing in front of a live audience again. We also wanted to find out how an audience would take to our original music. We had planned to invite around fifteen to twenty friends and fellow musicians to our gathering. Needless to say, word spread about the party, and by five o'clock in the afternoon, there were approximately fifty guests, mostly uninvited guests, prowling my basement and backyard.

We hadn't prepared for so many people, and it quickly became obvious that our meager supply of beer and munchies wasn't going to cut it for so many partygoers. Jeff took the lead on this problem and went from person to person taking up cash donations so we could buy more beer and party supplies. Thirty minutes later, Jeff drove off with a guy named Roger, who was the only person attending the party who had a pickup truck. They returned sometime later with two kegs of beer, a tap, and enough ice to keep the kegs cold for the duration of the party.

By then the number of guests attending our little soirée had swelled to over sixty, and I was becoming concerned that the commotion would rile the neighbors and attract the attention of local law enforcement. But as it turned out, all my worrying had been for naught. No police officers or angry neighbors ever showed up at my door.

Entropy took the stage (if you can call a basement a stage) around seven o'clock that evening, and the party and our performance ended up being a huge hit with our guests. The band made many new friends and fans that day, and we were all very pleased with the outcome. Well, with the exception of my house and yard being completely trashed, that is.

Later that same evening, after my bandmates had pitched in and helped me clean up the mess, Chuck, Jeff, and the few remaining stragglers called it a night and went their separate ways. Trice, L.B., and I stayed up late into the evening talking about music and anything else that happened to cross our minds. Before we knew it, it was well past three o'clock in the morning. Knowing that Trice and L.B. had a long drive to get back home, I offered to let them spend the night at my house. Trice had spent the night at my place many times in the past, but it would be a first for L.B.

Both of the guys were exhausted and accepted my offer without a second thought. L.B. headed off to sleep in the guest bedroom upstairs, I went to sleep in my bedroom, and Trice crashed on the living room couch. Early the next morning, Trice and I were awakened by the sound of laughter. L.B.'s laughter, to be precise.

Even from the solitude of the downstairs bedroom, the sound of L.B.'s laughter had roused me from my slumber. I sat up in bed and brushed the sleep from my eyes. I looked at the alarm clock. It was barely 6:30 in the morning. I had only been asleep for a few hours, and with all the activity the night before, I wasn't too happy about being awakened so early in the day. *What the hell is he going on about?* I remember thinking.

Still exhausted and feeling somewhat grouchy, I hastily threw back the covers and climbed out of bed. I walked into the living room and saw that Trice had also been awakened by the sound of L.B.'s laughter. Trice gave me a quick look and sat up on the couch. It was obvious that he was every bit as confused as I was about what our little drummer boy was up to. *Did he sneak a girl up there after Trice and I were asleep?* I wondered. But that didn't make any sense. As far as we knew, L.B. was alone in the bedroom, and he was well aware of the fact that if he wanted a girl to stay the night, all he had to do was ask. Trice got up from the couch, and the two of us went upstairs to find out what L.B. was so giddy about.

The door to the upstairs bedroom was slightly ajar, and through this slim opening we could see that L.B. was sitting up in bed and still laughing. He was holding an open book in his hands. A wild grin crossed his face. In contrast to the grin and the laughter, there was a strange, otherworldly look in his eyes. The combination was disturbing. The look on L.B.'s face was very similar to how Chuck had looked the night the gray man had appeared to us in the basement. So similar, in fact, that just looking at him sent a chill down my spine. L.B. turned his gaze from the book he was holding. He looked up at us, and his grin became even wider, making the otherworldly look in his eyes appear exaggerated. Trice pushed open the door, and the two of us stepped inside the room.

The upstairs bedroom was small but well laid out. There was a built-in desk filling a cubbyhole in the corner and a built-in vanity centered beneath three tall and slender windows. A twin-size canopy bed was also built into the architecture of the room. At the foot of the bed was a doorway that led to the attic. The doorway was very small and was more suitable for a dwarf or a hobbit than a full-grown human being.

For a reason I had never been able to put my finger on, I had always found that tiny door unsettling, and the attic that it led to even more so. Something about the door and the attic felt wrong. Wrong in a way that keeps a person awake at night with a severe case of the creeps. I had felt this way about the guest bedroom from the time I was a child and had personally never been able to sleep in that room without leaving it in the middle of the night to find other accommodations. Judging by the look on L.B.'s face, the guest bedroom had affected him in a similar way.

Stepping further into the room and sitting down on the edge of the bed, Trice asked L.B. what he was up to. L.B. didn't respond. He just sat there grinning.

"That must be one funny book you're reading," Trice said.

Still wide-eyed and grinning, L.B. responded by saying, "I dreamt this book last night."

"You mean you dreamt *about* the book?" I asked. I was confused by the statement.

"No," L.B. said, "I actually dreamt the book." He held the book up so Trice and I could get a better look at it. "I've never read it before, never even heard of it, but somehow I dreamt the entire story." Then L.B. placed the book in his lap and frowned. He shook his head. "No," he continued, "that isn't right. It was more than just a dream. It's like I was really there, like I was living the book."

L.B. went on to tell us that in his dream—if it really *had* been a dream—a shadowy male figure had appeared in the bedroom and told him the story exactly the way it was written in the book. "Like a movie playing out all around me," L.B. told us. The way that L.B. described the dream made it sound as though he himself was an integral part of the storyline—more of a character than an observer. The story in L.B.'s dream centered on an epic battle between ethereal beings and dark, supernatural forces. It was a classic battle between good and evil. L.B. went on to say that the man in his dream had told him that we (meaning the members of Entropy) would play a major role in a similar battle many years in the future and that Entropy was an important part of his plans.

"Which side will we be fighting for?" I jokingly asked.

L.B. smiled up at me but didn't answer the question. He then told us that the dream was by far the strangest, most vivid dream he'd ever had in his life and unlike any dream he'd ever had. L.B. admitted that the experience had left him shaken and yet extremely elated at the same time.

It was obvious to Trice and me that L.B. had experienced something out of the ordinary, but neither of us had a clue as to what or why. Needless to say, our day had started out strangely. But we hadn't seen anything yet. I wish that I could remember exactly what book it was that L.B. had dreamt about that night, but I'll be honest and tell you that I cannot remember. This little detail, like so many other details, was lost to me somewhere across the distance of time. But that doesn't really matter. What matters is that for a reason that I have never been able to fully comprehend, L.B.'s dream was pivotal to everything that followed.

The Ghost in the Machine, Part Two

Later that same morning, after the three of us had showered and were full of coffee and scraps of leftover munchies from the night before, we sat together on the couch in my living room, still listening to L.B. jabbering away about his dream. Sitting on an end table next to the couch was my old stereo system, a hand-me-down that my parents had given to me after I moved out on my own.

The stereo was a combo unit that contained a record player, an AM/FM radio, and a four-channel eight-track cassette player. The eight-track's channels were displayed on the face of the stereo by four lighted buttons numbered one through four. The eight-track player still had one of my mom's old cassettes jammed inside of it that no one had ever succeeded in getting unstuck. The eight-track hadn't worked in a number of years. As we sat on the couch talking, music from the stereo's FM radio was playing softly in the background. Our conversation was interrupted when the stereo began behaving as if it had been possessed by a demon.

The first strange thing the three of us heard was a series of three loud clicks coming from the stereo's speakers. Then the music playing over the radio began to swell and recede, getting louder and then softer, over and over again. We all leaned forward on the couch to get a look at the front of the stereo to see what was going on with it. As the three of us sat there watching, the stereo system started to go completely nuts.

The volume was consistently getting louder and then softer. The radio started changing channels as if an unseen hand was turning the dial. The stations started to fluctuate at random, changing from a clear signal to static and then to a different station altogether. Then the eight-track started playing for the first time in years. This wouldn't have been so strange in and of itself, but the eight-track was playing and sounding *at the same time* that the radio was playing and sounding. As far as I knew, this was impossible. Each component on the system had to be hand-selected to be able to be heard. Next, the eight-track's four channel display buttons began lighting up and changing on their own. The channels were changing in rapid succession, beginning with channel one and tracking through channel four and then back again, repeating the sequence—1, 2, 3, 4—over and over again.

By then, the three of us were no longer sitting on the couch. We were standing in front of the stereo staring at it like it wasn't a stereo at all, but rather an alien spacecraft that had just crash-landed in my living room. As we stood there watching, the channels on the eight-track started changing even faster—1, 2, 3, 4, over and over again, faster and faster, until they were nothing but a blur.

Just before the stereo system stopped functioning altogether and went dark, we heard two distinct words sound over the speakers. These words were "trust" and "me." Upon hearing these words, L.B.'s knees buckled and he almost went down on the floor. I'm certain that he would have gone down if Trice hadn't had the presence of mind to grab him by the arm and keep him from falling. I was confused by L.B.'s reaction. What we had just witnessed was unquestionably odd, but I thought L.B.'s response to a malfunctioning stereo system was a little over the top.

"What's wrong?" Trice asked as he guided our drummer back to the couch and helped him sit down. Trice appeared to be very concerned. Then I noticed the look on L.B.'s face, and I also became concerned. He was completely terrified of something. The only question was of *what*. I was about to ask him that very question, but Trice beat me to it. Trice had also noticed the look of terror on L.B.'s face. Trice shot me a quick glance and then turned his attention back to L.B. "What are you so afraid of?" Trice asked him.

"The stereo," L.B. managed to say, with a shaky voice. "Those words."

"Words?" I asked. "What words?" I glanced at the dead stereo. I suddenly understood what he was talking about. "Oh," I said, "You mean the words 'trust me'?" L.B. looked up at me and tried to smile. He nodded. I shrugged and asked, "What about them?"

"My dream last night," L.B. said. "Those were the last words the man in my dream spoke to me before I woke up."

I just stood there for a moment staring at L.B. I was trying to piece everything together in my mind. The dream had affected L.B. much more than I had realized. I now understood exactly what L.B. was trying to tell us. I understood why he was so terrified, but I didn't believe it. Or rather I didn't *want* to believe it. It was apparent that L.B. was convinced that there was a connection between the shadowy man in his dream and what had just happened with the stereo system. *That's just not possible*, I stood there thinking. I didn't want to admit to myself that such a thing was possible, even though I knew it was.

The rules in our little corner of the world had changed. The gray man had seen to that. I stared at the stereo system again and sighed. Other than my old black-and-white TV, the stereo was the only other source of electronic entertainment on the main level of the house. Still lying to myself that there was no link whatsoever between L.B.'s dream and the possessed stereo system, I walked upstairs to retrieve the clock radio from the guest bedroom. What happened while I was on my way back *down* the stairs vanquished all my remaining doubts.

When I reached the upstairs bedroom, I walked over to the dresser and unplugged the digital clock radio from the wall. I did this quickly because my uneasy feeling about the guest bedroom was stronger than ever, and I didn't feel comfortable being alone in the room. With clock in hand, I stepped outside the room and began descending the stairs. About halfway down, I saw that Trice was walking toward the landing at the bottom of the stairwell. He took a few steps up the stairs toward me and extended an open hand.

"Give it to me," he said. "We'll have to plug it in behind the stereo, and I can do it a lot easier than you can."

Trice was right. I stood six foot four and wore size ten and a half shoes. The combination of my lofty height and small feet made me terribly uncoordinated, and Trice knew it. He knew there was a better than fifty-fifty chance that if I tried to bend over the stereo to plug in the clock, I would become unbalanced and go crashing to the floor, taking the clock and stereo system with me.

Taking two more steps down the stairs, I extended the clock radio toward Trice. Just before he could take it from my hand, the radio turned on by itself and the numbers 3:33 flashed across the clock's digital face three times before going dark again. I was so startled by the unexpected sound that I jerked back my arm as if I had just touched a hot stove. The clock radio fell from my hand. It went crashing to the stair beneath my feet, rolled past Trice, and came to rest on the landing behind him. Trice shook his head and shot me an aggravated look. This gave me pause. Trice's reaction was way out of character, but I attributed it to the exhausting activity of the day before.

"Now it's probably as broken as the stereo system is," he said, sounding every bit as aggravated as he looked. Trice turned, knelt down, and picked up the clock radio from the landing. "What the hell was that, anyway?" he asked me. "Did the clock's battery backup kick in or what?"

Trice turned the radio over in his hands to examine it. He quickly discovered what I already knew. The clock radio *didn't have* a battery backup. The only way it would work is if it were plugged into an electrical socket. Trice turned his head and looked up at me, shocked. He stretched out his arms, holding the clock radio away from his chest as though any second it might come to life and rip him apart.

"It doesn't take a battery," he told me.

"I know," I said.

"Then how in the hell could that have possibly happened?" he asked me. "How could it have turned on without any power?"

The question was rhetorical. There was no possible way that the clock and the radio could turn on without being plugged into a wall socket, and Trice knew it. He just stood there in silence, staring intently at the device. Finally, Trice turned away from me and took the last few steps down the stairs. Just before his foot came down on the landing, the old rotary dial telephone sitting on a desk a few feet away from him started ringing. The sound of the phone startled Trice. He lost his balance, and the clock radio slipped from his hands and went crashing down on the stairs for a second time.

Trice threw up his arms in exasperation and shouted, "I got it!" He stormed over to the desk to answer the phone, leaving the clock radio lay where it had come to rest on the stairs. He answered the phone on the third ring.

"Hello?" Trice said. He listened carefully for a short time, then placed the receiver back onto its cradle without saying another word. He snatched his car keys from off the desk where he had left them the night before.

"So?" I asked. "Who was it?"

"I'm not sure," Trice said without looking in my direction. He was still staring down at the phone. "It was pretty much nothing but static, but just for a second I thought I heard someone talking."

"Well?" I asked. "What did they say?"

After a long pause, Trice said, "I'm not going to answer that right now. I'm going for a drive. I'll be back later."

Trice walked over to the front door. He opened it, stepped across the threshold, and slammed the door shut behind him. From the living room couch, L.B. started laughing again. Feeling as helpless as a babe in the woods, I just stood there on the stairs. I'd never heard laughter that sounded so lost.

By the time Trice returned, Chuck and Jeff had shown up together at my house. L.B. had already told them about the strange dream he'd had the night before, and I had described the incident with the stereo and the clock radio. Trice appeared to be in a much better mood than he'd been in before leaving the house so abruptly earlier in the day. Trice sat down in the living room with the rest of us and joined in on the conversation. He gave Chuck and Jeff his side of the story.

After a lengthy discussion on the subject, it became clear that the bizarre events we had been experiencing were growing in both frequency and intensity. It was equally clear that it was time to admit to ourselves and one other that whatever was haunting us had no intentions of simply closing up shop and moving on. There was an unexplainable presence surrounding the five of us. There was a force at work that none of us had the mental or spiritual tools to comprehend. If we were going to figure out what the gray man was and what he wanted from us, this clearly had to change.

After hearing us out, Chuck admitted to us that he'd been experiencing a bizarre phenomenon that he couldn't explain away. Over the last two weeks, he'd been waking up late in the night for no apparent reason and at very specific times. He explained to us that the first night it happened he had awoken at exactly 3:33 in the morning. On other nights he had awoken at such times as 11:11, 2:22, and 4:44. Chuck explained to us that he was typically a very heavy sleeper and that for him to wake up in the middle of the night was a rare event.

Chuck had been quite interested in hearing about what we had experienced earlier in the day, the experience with the clock radio in particular, and now we understood why he had been so interested. When the clock radio had turned on by itself on the stairway, it had flashed the numbers 3:33 three times before going dark again. It suddenly occurred to me that the telephone had rung exactly three times before Trice had answered it. I had no idea if these two things were related, but I found the possibility fascinating nonetheless.

I also recalled two more things that I believed could possibly be related to the phenomena we had been experiencing with time and numbers. The first thing I remembered was that one of the definitions of entropy had something to do with linear time. I had mentioned this to Jeff and Chuck the night I had come up with the name for the band. I made a mental note to get out an encyclopedia and dictionary sometime soon and look up the word entropy. The second thing I remembered was that immediately after Chuck, Jeff, and I had encountered the gray man in the basement, the time was exactly 11:11 PM. I knew this for a fact because there was a clock on the fireplace mantle, and I had looked at it just before we ran up the basement stairs.

And lastly, I remembered that on the day that Trice and I had gotten stranded alongside the road with a flat tire, I had awakened from my trance at exactly 3:33 in the afternoon. That was also the day that I had informed my bandmates that the gray man had given me the poem while Trice and I had been walking home. *The poem*, I thought to myself. I told the guys to hang on for a minute. I ran to my bedroom to retrieve the poem from the dresser where I had stashed it many weeks earlier. Returning to the living room with the poem in hand, I stood in front of my bandmates and read it aloud for the second time.

Feel the force of life surrounds us, every fiber, every strand. Don't fear for I will be here with us, conquest conquer, living sands. Swirling mists again surround us, forever time, time at hand. Strange spaces, traces, empty faces, reach now for the gifts upon the land.

After reading it again, I realized that the poem also contained a reference to time. Up to this point, I had taken the poem at face value. It was just a poem, I had told myself, a poem and nothing more. But now I wasn't so sure. Now I wondered if there was something below the surface of the words that I just wasn't seeing.

After everyone else had gone home for the evening, I asked Trice for a second time what he had heard over the telephone, and for a second time he refused to talk about it. Many months would pass before he finally confided in me.

The Room of Lost Dreams, Part Two
November 1980

Shelby Martin was eighteen years old and a senior in high school on the day I met her. So was her best friend, Janice Goen. Shortly after L.B.'s dream and the incident with the stereo system, Trice had started dating Janice and I had started dating Shelby. The girls were very attractive and the perfect arm candy for two aspiring rock musicians.

Shelby and Janice lived in a small town called Loveland, which was situated between where Trice lived in Boulder and where I lived in Fort Collins. I had hit it off quite well with Shelby's parents, and even though Shelby and I had only been dating for a short time and she was still in high school, they allowed their daughter to stay over at my place on weekends. Shelby had a deep love for animals, an affinity she unfortunately didn't share with her parents. They didn't allow animals of any kind in their home. But, of course, as is so often the case with smart and attractive young women, Shelby wasn't about to let that stop her.

One Saturday morning after I had picked up Shelby at her house and we were making the short drive to Fort Collins, she spied an old, rusted-out pickup truck sitting in the parking lot of an abandoned gas station. Taped to the truck's tailgate was a sign that read "Free Kittens." I had seen the truck and the sign first and hoped that Shelby wouldn't notice them. But as fate would have it, Shelby did notice the sign and the truck, and I knew full well what was coming next. Shelby was getting a brand-new kitten, and it was going to live with me. There was no getting around it.

Now if you're wondering what girlfriends and kittens have to do with a rock 'n' roll band and an otherworldly entity, please bear with me. I promise you won't be disappointed. I should also tell you that even though Shelby and I had learned a great deal about each other during the few weeks we'd been together, at the time she knew absolutely nothing about the gray man or any of the other strange happenings the members of Entropy had been experiencing over the previous four months.

Before Shelby even got around to asking, I pulled the Camaro into the gas station and parked next to the pickup truck. She was absolutely delighted, and it pleased me to see her so happy. Shelby was so happy, in fact, that she was out of the car and at the back of the truck perusing the selection of felines before I even had a chance to kill the Camaro's engine. Ten minutes later, Shelby was back inside the car with a tiger-striped ball of fluff sitting on her lap. I was happy, Shelby was happy, and I figured I might even get a little sex out of the deal. Boy, was I wrong!

Shelby had a particular quirk that she shared with her mother. This quirk would change the outcome of the entire evening. Later that same night as we were getting ready for bed, Shelby pointed out to me that we had a little problem. The problem had to do with her new kitten and the box fan in my bedroom. Shelby, like her mother, found it impossible to fall asleep without a fan running in the room. I personally believed that this had more to do with the noise than the air-flow, but facts were facts and there was nothing I could do to change it.

The problem we were facing was that my box fan (the only fan in the house at the time, I might add) was missing the back cover that kept anything from getting into the fan's spinning blades. Shelby was certain that her new kitten would jump off the bed in the middle of the night and innocently wander into the back of the fan and be killed. I suggested that the problem was an easy fix and that I could simply set the fan off the floor on a chair or on top of the dresser. But stubbornly, Shelby wouldn't hear of it. She was concerned that the fan's vibration might cause it to fall off a chair or the dresser and crush her kitten beneath it. I figured Shelby's assessment of the situation was complete bullshit, but as I've already pointed out, men are typically hopeless in fighting the will of beautiful young women, and I knew there and then that I was pretty much screwed.

But even more aggravating was Shelby's solution to our little problem. She was resolved to have me spend the night in the master bedroom with the kitten and for her to sleep in the guest bedroom upstairs with the fan. Upon hearing Shelby's plan, I briefly considered heading out on the streets in search of a new fan, but by then it was approaching midnight, and I knew that this wasn't a plausible fix. In those days, we didn't have twenty-four-hour mega-marts like we do now, at least not in my neck of the woods, and my chances of finding a store that was still open that sold fans were slim to none. I was getting very tired by that point anyway and didn't feel up to arguing about it further. Shelby and I were going to spend the night in separate bedrooms, and there was nothing I could do to change that. I grabbed the fan and guided Shelby upstairs to the guest bedroom.

After Shelby was safely tucked into bed and I had given her a kiss, I headed back downstairs to sleep with the kitten. As I closed the guest room door behind me, I couldn't help but think about L.B. and his dream.

A little before two o'clock in the morning, I was awakened by a whispered voice and a soft touch on the arm. It was Shelby, and after my eyes had adjusted to the dim light in the bedroom, I could see that she didn't look happy. In fact, she looked very concerned. Shelby took me by the hand and said, "I need you to come upstairs with me. There are some really weird things happening in the bedroom and I need you to check it out. I don't think I can sleep up there anymore."

"Weird like how?" I asked as I sat up in bed.

"You're going to have to go up and see for yourself," she said. "It isn't something I can explain with just words."

Shelby let go of my hand and picked up her kitten from off the bed. She cradled it tightly to her breast. I got out of bed and followed her upstairs to the guest bedroom. Along the way, my imagination took on a life of its own. What would I see up there?

Reaching the landing at the bottom of the stairs, I looked up. I saw that the door to the guest bedroom was standing wide open and that the light in the small entryway just outside the room was on. Shelby saw this too. "I closed the bedroom door behind me," she said. "I'm certain of it."

"Okay, okay," I said in the steadiest voice I could manage. I somehow kept my cool even though I had a very uneasy feeling. "Don't freak out on me," I warned her. "Let's just get up there so you can show me what happened."

Shelby and I climbed the stairs side by side, looking and listening intently as we went. When we reached the landing at the top of the stairs, I took a good look around the guest room. I could see nothing out of the ordinary. Other than the disheveled bedclothes, nothing appeared to be out of place. Stepping inside the room, I shrugged and said, "Okay, so what happened?"

Shelby walked over to the bed and motioned for me to join her there. "Over here," she said. "Come sit next to me on the bed." "Oh," she quickly added, "close the door first, okay?"

"Okay." I reached for the bedroom door and closed it behind me. With the door closed, it was very dark inside the room, but there was just enough moonlight filtering in through the windows over the vanity for me to see my way. Moving carefully in Shelby's direction, I crossed the room and sat down next to her on the bed.

"Now watch," Shelby said.

"Watch what?" I asked.

"There." She raised her hand and pointed toward the small door leading to the attic. "The wall next to that little door," she continued. "Just watch it."

I did watch. I could see nothing but the dimly lit door and the wall. "I don't see anything," I said. I started to ask Shelby exactly what it was I was supposed to be looking for, but I cut off my own words mid-sentence. As I sat on the bed watching, a greenish glow slowly appeared on the wall next to the attic door. I could soon see that the glow was in the shape of a handprint. Even though I'd experienced some crazy shit over the previous few months, a glowing handprint was a little too Hollywood for me. I wasn't buying it. "It has to be something explainable," I said. "Phosphorescent paint or something. You know, the glow-in-the-dark stuff you can buy at a variety store." I turned my head and glanced over my shoulder at the three windows behind me. "It could just be moonlight shining in through the windows. Or maybe it's the street-light on the corner." I stood up from the bed, reached over the vanity, and closed the shades and curtains. I turned around and looked at the wall. The glowing handprint was still there. If anything, it was even brighter than before.

"Glow-in-the-dark paint it is," I said. I walked over to the wall to get a closer look. Now there was no mistaking it. The glow was definitely in the shape of a handprint. I could even make out individual lines in the palm. I lifted my right hand and placed it directly over the handprint on the wall. The handprint disappeared. I was certain that I had identified the culprit. I was just about to say so when the glowing handprint reappeared. But this time the handprint wasn't on the wall. It was on the back of my *own hand*. I jerked my hand away from the wall and took two steps backward. The glowing handprint slowly reappeared on the wall exactly where it had been when I first saw it.

"Okay," I said to Shelby without turning to face her. I was still staring intently at the wall. As I watched, the handprint faded and vanished completely, leaving behind no traces that it had ever been there. "Let's get the hell out of here," I said. What happened next unfolded in less than ten seconds' time.

I turned away from the wall and stepped over to the fan. Kitten or no kitten, I knew Shelby would want the fan downstairs. As I did this, Shelby stood up from where she was sitting on the bed. Her new kitten was still safely cradled in her arms. Shelby walked over to the bedroom door and opened it. The guest room flooded with light from the entryway. Squinting from the sudden flash of light, I reached behind the fan and unplugged it from the wall. As I was wrapping the cord in my hands, Shelby let out a shriek. In a voice thick with immediacy, she cried out, "Oh my God, Marcus! Look!"

I looked up from my work. I could see only the open doorway and the entryway beyond it. Both were empty. I looked at Shelby. She was standing just inside the room. She was looking at neither the doorway nor the entryway, but at the wall behind me. Her face and eyes shone with the light of terror. I turned around and looked at the wall. I saw Shelby's shadow and my own shadow. Between our shadows was a third shadow. The third shadow was in the shape of a man. It was monstrous and hulking.

My body ran wild with gooseflesh. I nervously looked all around the tiny room. I could see only Shelby and her kitten. I looked back at the open door and the entryway. Still empty. There was nothing there, nothing that could account for the third shadow on the wall. I turned sharply on my heels and faced the wall again. As I watched, the shadow—which I knew wasn't a shadow at all but something impossible—grew larger and larger, blacker and blacker, until it enveloped the entire wall and most of the ceiling. I heard a sharp click as the latch on the attic door released and it swung open. I snapped my head in the direction of the noise. The glowing handprint was back, but it was no longer on the wall. Now it was in the center of the attic door. I could hear whispered voices coming from the darkness beyond it. I turned and rushed toward Shelby. I grabbed her by the arm and pushed her from the room. The voices coming from the attic grew louder as I slammed the door shut behind me.

I managed to stay close behind Shelby as she ran down the stairs. Bolting into the living room and stopping to catch my breath, I saw that she had made it out of the bedroom with the kitten and I had somehow made it out with the fan. But this wasn't surprising considering I had the fan's handle in a death grip. We were both shaking uncontrollably, but that didn't matter. For the moment, all that mattered was that we were out of that god-awful room. All that mattered was that we were safe.

But Shelby was terrified, and rightfully so. I knew that I only had a few precious seconds before she would ask me what was happening in my house. I had to quickly decide how much of the truth I was going to tell her. *But was this even the same thing?* I wondered. *Was the presence in the guest room the gray man? Or was it something else?*

Even though I was reasonably certain that it *was* the gray man, this time the entity felt different than it had before. This time the gray man's talk-show-host persona had been shed for something unquestionably darker, something that was possibly even malevolent. But my gut told me that this new incident had more to do with Shelby than with me. My gut told me that the gray man didn't care for Shelby being in that room. Not one bit. Had the gray man intentionally put on a show to try to frighten Shelby? If that had been the gray man's intention, it had certainly worked.

As I stood there deep in thought and mulling things over in my mind, the inevitable happened. Shelby stepped up close to me and asked, "What happened up there, Marcus? I...I don't understand. Where did those voices come from? What made the handprint and that awful shadow on the wall?"

I hesitated before answering. My mind was racing with broken thoughts and images. I was still trying to piece together what had happened and how much of the story I should spill. *If I tell her the truth,* I wondered, *will she think I'm a nutcase? A crackpot? Will she pack her bags and walk out of my life forever?* As I much as I didn't want to lose Shelby as a girlfriend, I decided to roll the dice. I gambled that telling her the truth would put the terrifying apparitions we had both witnessed in the upstairs bedroom in a context that she could understand.

That night I told Shelby everything. I told her about my trance and the poem that I had been given. I told her about the gray man. I told her about the numbers and even about the stereo system and the clock radio. I told her the truth and hoped that she would believe me and stay by my side. Thankfully, she did believe me. Shelby told me that before her grandmother died, she had told Shelby about similar ghostly experiences she'd had as a child. Shelby said that her grandmother believed that the house she had grown up in was haunted and that ghosts were every bit as real as living people. She went on to tell me that even though she'd never personally seen a ghost or had a paranormal experience before then, she had always believed that they existed.

Hearing this from Shelby was a huge relief. Even though we were both still feeling the after-effects of what we had experienced, her words were inexplicably soothing. I took Shelby by the hand, and before I knew it, we were snuggled in my bed and falling asleep. Shelby's kitten (which she had yet to name) was curled up next to her chest, and the fan was propped up on a chair and gently humming. This was a good thing. I was filled with relief that we had made it out of the upstairs bedroom with the kitten and the fan. There was no way I was going back in that room. Not tonight, anyway. Just before I closed my eyes for the last time that evening, I glanced at the alarm clock sitting on the table next to my bed. It was 12:34 AM.

That same night, I had a disturbing dream. Well, at least that's the way it felt the next morning when I woke up. My memories of the dream were vague at best. All I really remembered about the dream was that it had something to do with the framed Winslow Homer print hanging on the wall in my living room. I briefly considered telling Shelby about the dream, but then thought better of it. There was no point in telling her. I barely remembered the dream anyway, and after the events of the night before, I knew that piling more on Shelby's shoulders was a bad idea.

A few hours later, I drove Shelby back to Loveland and then went the store to pick up a litter pan and some food for the kitten. I was exhausted and irritable. The strangeness that had pervaded my life was starting to take its toll on me. While I was shopping, I couldn't help but wonder how long it would be before the bell would ring and the next round of madness would begin.

The Horn

Three days had passed since Shelby and I had seen the unexplainable shadow and the handprints in the guest bedroom. Three days since I'd had the dream, a dream that I couldn't quite remember and yet for some unknown reason was deeply disturbing to me. I hadn't gotten much sleep the last three days, and I was still very much on edge.

It was a Wednesday night. I had to work the next morning, so I decided to get to bed early to try to catch up on my sleep. I had only been asleep for a few hours when I was jolted awake by the sound of a horn blasting in my ear. The sound was so loud and abrupt that upon hearing it I literally jumped up and out of my bed in a single motion. I just stood there next to my bed in the darkness, somewhere between asleep and awake, trying to figure out what had made the sound.

The horn blast had been a single note. It was the sound of a brass wind instrument, maybe a saxophone or possibly even a trumpet. The horn had sounded from somewhere inside my bedroom, somewhere very close to my ear. I was certain of it. I was convinced that the horn had been a real sound and not a remnant of a dream. After I jumped out of bed, I could still hear the sound of the horn reverberating inside the room.

I walked over to the closet and flicked on the light switch. I looked all around but could see nothing unusual.

I left the bedroom and walked through the main level of the house. Again, there was nothing unusual or out of place. The clock radio wasn't playing and the television set was dark. There was nothing running in the house that could account for the noise. I was far too tired to think about it further, so I walked to my bedroom and went back to sleep.

I awoke the next morning to the realization that for the last five nights I'd been having the exact same dream. It was the same dream I'd had the night that Shelby and I had encountered the gray man in the upstairs bedroom. Even though I'd been having the same dream for five nights in a row, I still couldn't remember exactly what the dream was about. All I could remember was that it had something to do with the Winslow Homer print hanging on the wall in my living room. I got out of bed, showered, had a quick bite to eat, and went to work.

Later that night as I lay sleeping in bed, I was again jolted awake by the sound of a horn blasting in my ear. I sat straight up in bed. The sound had startled me so badly that my hands were shaking and I had a hard time catching my breath. Once I calmed down, I searched the dark bedroom with my eyes but could see nothing. I looked at the clock sitting on the table next to the bed. It was 11:34 PM. It was the first time in days that I had looked at a clock without seeing sequential numbers. For the second time in as many nights, I got out of bed and walked through the main level of the house. I still couldn't find anything unusual or out of place. I returned to my bedroom and went back to sleep.

For the next six nights in a row, I was haunted by the sound of a horn blasting in my ear and jolting me from my sleep. But now things had changed. Now, without exception, the horn was waking me up every night at exactly 3:33 in the morning. I was starting to lose it. I was teetering on the edge of extreme fatigue, and I was even questioning my own sanity. I wasn't eating right or taking care of myself. I knew that if I couldn't figure out a way to make the dream and the horn stop that I was going to end up in the hospital or an insane asylum, or both.

Many times over the last week I had considered telling my bandmates what was happening to me. But I didn't tell them. Nor did I tell Shelby. I was missing work and on the verge of losing my job. I started making up excuses to postpone band rehearsals and to avoid spending time with my girlfriend. I can't tell you exactly why I started doing these things because even I didn't know why I was doing them. But I did know that things had to change, and they had to change soon.

I decided to start sleeping on the living room couch to see if it made any difference. Much to my relief, it did make a difference. My first night sleeping on the couch was peaceful. I slept through the entire night without waking up once. No horn blasting in my ear, no disturbances of any kind. I woke up the next morning feeling better than I had in days. But it was short-lived. The very next night as I lay sleeping on the couch, I was awakened at exactly 3:33 AM by the sound of the horn blasting in my ear.

I was getting desperate. I was willing to do whatever it took to make the horn stop. Well, with the exception of spending the night in the guest room, that is. I just couldn't resign myself to sleeping in that room. Not by myself, anyway, and I had no intention of inviting Shelby to spend the night with me while this was going on.

Desperate for answers, I decided to go to the Fort Collins library and pick up some books about ghosts, the paranormal, and numerology. I also wanted to see if the library had any books available on the subject of entropy. After arriving at the library and searching the shelves, I sat down at a table in a secluded corner with an impressive stack of books. I spent the rest of the day poring through the text in search of answers.

Unfortunately, the number of books my local library carried about ghosts was slim, and the few I had picked from the shelves were practically useless for my needs. There was very little useful information in them. The books about ghosts made for interesting reads, and in reading them I learned a great deal about different types of ghosts and hauntings, but there was no relevant information in the text. There were no references to apparitions of gray men or rings of blue fire. There was no mention of glowing handprints or ghostly horns. It quickly became obvious that the paranormal events my bandmates and I had been experiencing were far more advanced than anything covered in the books that were available at my local library.

In stark contrast, the books I read on numerology contained a wealth of useful information, and the single volume I found on the topic of entropy would prove to be invaluable in the months to come. While I was reading, I jotted down copious notes. When I finished, I placed the books about ghosts back on the shelves and checked out two books about numerology and the book about entropy. Those books contained good and useful information. Unfortunately, for the time being, that information did absolutely nothing to stop the dreaming or prevent the horn from waking me up in the middle of the night.

Over the next ten days, I was awakened every night at exactly 3:33 in the morning by the sound of the horn blasting in my ear. By then I had tried sleeping in every room in the house in an effort to get the horn and the dream to stop, but nothing changed. I tried sleeping on the couch again, but to no avail. I tried sleeping in my bedroom and in the basement. One night I even tried sleeping in the bathtub, but that didn't work either. Nothing I did stopped the horn and the dream—a dream that I still couldn't remember after I had woken up.

One night I tried sleeping on the living room couch again. At 3:33 AM I was jolted awake by the sound of the horn blasting in my ear. I sat up on the couch. I sat there in the darkness feeling like my entire life had become nothing more than a nightmare of insanity and confusion. I got up off the couch and walked to the center of the living room. I'd had all I could take. At the top of my voice I screamed, "What the fuck do you want from me?!" I really didn't expect an answer, but I got one anyway. The stereo system that had lain dormant for many weeks powered up on its own. The eight-track's third channel lit up and slowly flashed three times before the stereo system went dark again.

At that moment I remembered the dream. At least I remembered the beginning and the ending of the dream. The middle of the dream was still vague. I could recall emotions and random images about the middle of the dream, but little else. But for the moment that didn't matter. My memories of the beginning and the ending of the dream were intact. I now knew what had to be done. At least I was pretty sure I knew.

I looked around the living room one last time. I looked at the stereo system and saw that it was still dark. I walked to the bedroom, curled up in my own bed, and slept through the rest of the night. In the morning I called Chuck and told him that if at all possible I needed to see him right away. Chuck said that he had planned to spend the morning just hanging out around his house and didn't have anything major going on at the moment. He said that he would head over right away.

Chuck showed up at my house at a little past ten o'clock in the morning. The first thing he told me after I opened the front door and greeted him was that I looked like shit.

I nodded in acknowledgment and told him thank you. I'd been through hell over the past month and I knew it showed. I told Chuck that we had a lot to talk about and invited him to come and sit with me in the living room.

The first thing I told Chuck was that I owed him and the rest of the guys an apology. I told him that I was very sorry for the way I had been acting lately. Then I told him exactly why I'd been acting so strangely. I told him about what Shelby and I had experienced in the guest room. I told him about the horn and the dream, but at the time I didn't tell him the exact details of the dream. I reminded him about the stereo and the numbers I had been seeing on the clock.

Chuck listened carefully to everything I had to say. After I had finished speaking, Chuck told me that he had also been seeing sequential numbers on a regular basis. "I haven't heard any horns or anything like that," he told me, "but I've also still been waking up in the middle of the night and seeing numbers like 10:10, 3:33, and 5:55 every damn time I turn around." He went on to tell me that even though he was seeing numbers repeatedly, and had been for quite some time, he had no idea why he had been noticing them or what any of it meant.

I told Chuck that I thought I had a pretty good idea why we had been seeing the numbers. I told him that I believed the numbers were a numerical, or possibly even a mathematical, language that the gray man had been using in an attempt to "speak" to us. But I also pointed out that the problem with my theory was that even if I was right, this was a language we didn't understand. "Right now the gray man might as well be speaking to us in ancient Egyptian," I told him.

Next I told Chuck about my trip to the library and the books I had studied. I showed him the generous notes I had taken, and we discussed some of the more interesting things I had noted during my reading. I told Chuck that while I was studying, I had learned that in the language of numerology, 3s have a variety of meanings. These meanings included transition, change, and travel, and (of most interest to me) "waking up," either physically or spiritually. I told Chuck that I had learned that in the context of repeating numbers, the number 33 represents generosity and the act of giving, although the gift is never a material object but rather the gift of knowledge, wisdom, faith, or love. I explained that according to the books I had read about numerology, if a person repeatedly sees sequential numbers on a clock, the license plates on cars, and so on, that they are being guided by a supernatural force.

I had also learned that the number 333 represented the "highest of beings." I explained to Chuck that these beings are oftentimes entities that possess extreme supernatural abilities and powers and that these entities may or may not be divine. As a supernatural power, I had read, the entity can transform itself into a doorway that leads to and from different dimensions. I explained that such a doorway is useless and meaningless to a person who cannot attain the correct state of mind to activate its power. And lastly, I told Chuck that one of the books I had read on numerology had referenced a biblical verse that was relevant to my situation. I knew that this verse would mean very little to Chuck, but because of the implications of the verse and its relationship to what I had been experiencing over the previous few weeks, it was very meaningful to me. The verse was taken from Ezekiel 33:3 and it read: "If, when he sees the sword coming on the land, by sounding the horn he gives people news of their danger."

I was uncertain about what Chuck would make of what I had just told him. Even after what Chuck, Jeff, and I had witnessed in the basement months earlier, I was worried that my friend might write me off as a lunatic. But much to my surprise and relief, Chuck seemed genuinely interested in this new information about numerology and supernatural forces. And as it turned out, I also hadn't given Chuck enough credit about recognizing the connection with the Bible verse and the horn. He had instantly recognized the connection and wanted to know more.

"Just so I'm clear," Chuck said, "nothing like this has ever happened to you before now?"

"That's right," I answered.

"No history of sleepwalking? No sleep disorders?"

I shook my head. "No."

"And the horn," he continued, "the horn wasn't real, right? The sound, I mean. The horn was just a part of the dream?"

I smiled at Chuck, but there was no joy in my smile. "That's the best part," I said. "At first I thought the sound was a real horn, but I started questioning it so I decided to do a little experiment." I stood up from where I was sitting on the couch and motioned for Chuck to follow me. "It's easier to just show you," I said. "Come with me to the basement."

Chuck and I walked through the kitchen, headed down the stairs, and entered the main room of the basement. As always, our musical equipment filled the center of the room and the two red couches lined the opposite wall. I walked over to the couches and began telling Chuck the details of the night I had slept in the basement. I told him that after I started hearing the horn, I had slept everywhere in the house I could to try to get it to stop. I explained that the first night I tried sleeping in the basement, I had decided to try to catch the sound of the horn on an audio recorder. The longest tape I could find for my portable cassette recorder was only sixty minutes long, and since the horn always woke me at 3:33 in the morning, I would have had to stay up until at least two thirty in the morning to start recording. If I'd started recording any earlier than that, the cassette deck would have run out of tape before the horn sounded. I told Chuck that after weeks of interrupted sleep, I was far too exhausted to stay up that late at night.

I walked across the room and over to where our band equipment was sitting and said, "So I decided to use this." I rested my hand on top of the reel-to-reel tape recorder that was sitting on a table next to my guitar amplifier.

My father had gifted me with the recorder a few years earlier. I typically used it to record the band's rehearsals or song ideas I came up with. I explained to Chuck that the tapes I had for the reel-to-reel were long enough to record for almost four hours if the machine was switched to its slowest setting. I told him that the night I had slept in the basement, I had managed to stay awake until just before midnight. Before I crashed out on the couch, I had adjusted the reel-to-reel recorder to its slowest setting and started recording.

"So were you able to catch the sound of the horn on audio?" Chuck asked.

I flipped the reel-to-reel's power switch to the on position and said, "When I listened to the tape the next morning I heard this." I pushed the play button. For the first ten seconds, all that came out over the reel-to-reel's speakers was a faint hiss. Then Chuck heard the same sound I'd been hearing over and over again for weeks. Over the recorder's speakers, a tremendous horn blast sounded. I didn't so much as flinch, but Chuck was startled by the suddenness of the sound. He frowned, took two steps closer to the recorder and me, and said, "Back that up and play it again." I pressed another button, rewound the tape, and pushed play. The blast of the horn sounded over the speakers for a second time.

Chuck bobbed his head. "Okay, okay," he said. He gestured to me with his hands, signaling me to kill the playback. I reached down and pressed the stop button. "That was definitely a trumpet," he told me. "I must have heard that same note hundreds of times when I was playing guitar for the high school jazz band. There's no mistaking it."

Chuck looked me in the eyes and shook his head. "So what the hell does all of this mean?"

"I don't know," I said, "but I can tell you this much. I'm sick of being terrorized by this thing. I'm sick of running from it."

Chuck nodded his head. He understood. "Then maybe we should try making contact with it," he said, "and figure out what it wants from us"

"Agreed," I said.

But how were we supposed to do that? If the gray man was trying to get our attention, it had certainly worked, but even if I was right about the numbers being a form of communication, we didn't have the slightest idea how to speak the language. The problem remained: how were we supposed to communicate with an entity from another world? In hopes of discovering an answer to this question, Chuck asked me to tell him more about the recurring dream I'd been having. He wanted to know everything. He asked me to tell him about the dream and to spare no detail. So we sat down together on one of the couches in the basement, and I told him.

The Dream

The dream was always the same, the location familiar. At least the beginning of the dream was familiar. When the dream began, I was standing in my living room in front of the framed Winslow Homer print that hung on the wall between the front door and the landing at the bottom of the stairs. The print was taken from one of Homer's original paintings and was titled "Breezing Up." The print featured a small sailboat sailing out to sea from the mouth of a harbor. Aboard the ship were three young boys and an old man with a gray beard. At one time the print had belonged to my grandfather, and I had always admired its simplistic beauty.

In my dream, as I stood there admiring the print, a dense mist filled the living room and swirled throughout the room. The mist felt ancient and primordial. A strong wind began blowing outside the house, stirring the living room curtains. The mist grew so dense I could no longer see the world around me. I was no longer certain where I was. I started feeling my consciousness being pulled away from my body. I was floating, being pulled further away and deeper into the mist. I could soon see hazy outlines in the distance, but the mist was still too thick to make out what the outlines were.

The next thing I knew, I was no longer floating through the mist. I was standing on a shoreline under a fiery-red sunset and looking out to sea. In the distance I could see a small sailboat as it sailed from the mouth of a harbor. It was the very same harbor that was in the Winslow Homer print. A warm summer breeze flowed across the water, caressing my skin and filling my nostrils with the smells of the harbor and salt from the sea. I could hear the sound of gulls complaining in the distance and the waves washing along the shoreline. It reminded me of my childhood and the vacations my parents would take my sister and me on to Macatawa Bay and the beaches of Lake Michigan. I could hear the familiar sound of a foghorn from a nearby lighthouse and the clanging of bells from buoys gently rocking in the wake…

It was at this point that the details of the dream became vague. The middle of the dream was mostly lost to me. Even though I could remember very little about the middle of the dream, I told Chuck that I had gotten the impression that I was out at sea, sailing across an ocean to a foreign land. I told him that I had the impression that the middle of the dream centered on a real life event that I would experience sometime in the future. I told Chuck I believed that the middle of the dream was unclear because my future was unclear. Right or wrong, I believed that my future wasn't written in stone, so neither was that part of the dream. Yes, the middle of the dream was vague, but the ending certainly wasn't. In my mind, the ending of the dream was every bit as crisp and vivid as the beginning.

At the end of the dream, I was once again standing on the shoreline and looking out to sea. But now I was no longer standing beneath a fiery-red sunset. The landscape was dark, and the sea was black. They were nighttime waters. Storm clouds were billowing on the horizon, and a dense, swirling mist was moving into the harbor across the surface of the water. The mist became so thick that I could no longer see the shoreline or anything else around me. I once again felt my consciousness being pulled away from my body. As I was being pulled further and further away, I could see the hazy outline of a large man floating alongside me through the mist.

When the mist finally cleared, I was standing in my own living room staring at the Winslow Homer print hanging on the wall. In my left hand I was holding a pencil and the piece of paper on which I had written the poem the day Trice and I had become stranded alongside the road. In my right hand I was holding a trumpet. I turned away from the print and walked up the stairs and into the guest room. Someone was asleep in the bed. I walked over to the bed to see who it was.

I set the pencil and the piece of paper on the vanity next to the bed. I set the trumpet on the floor at my feet. I picked up the pencil and added two new lines to the end of the poem. I put down the pencil and picked up the trumpet. I turned and faced the bed. I reached down and pulled back the covers. The person sleeping beneath the covers was me. I leaned over the bed and held the trumpet close to the sleeping man's ear. I pressed my lips hard against the mouthpiece and blew. In that moment the dream ended.

Chuck leaned back on the couch. A minute later he turned to face me and said, "Weird. So in the dream you were blowing the trumpet in your own ear?"

"Yes," I said. "And no."

It was difficult to put into words, but I managed to explain to Chuck that only a small part of the man holding the trumpet in the dream had been me. In the dream it had felt like my consciousness was in someone else's body. The man in the dream was me, and yet inexplicably he wasn't me. I explained to Chuck that at the end of the dream, I had no control over what my body was doing. It felt like I was merely observing the world around me through someone else's eyes.

After I had explained things to Chuck, I shrugged and said, "It was only a dream."

"Don't play stupid with me," Chuck replied. His voice was thick with sarcasm. "It was more than just a dream and you know it. I can see it in your eyes."

I just sat there on the couch in silence. Chuck was right. It was more than just a dream. Much more. I was exhausted and my mind was beyond frazzled. I had tried my best to avoid admitting to myself what I knew to be true.

Chuck placed his hand gently on my shoulder. In a much nicer tone of voice he said, "You also mentioned that in the dream you wrote down two new lines at the end of the poem, right?"

I nodded.

"Do you remember what those two lines were?"

"Yes."

"And do you still have the poem?"

I nodded again. "Yes, it's in the dresser in my bedroom."

Chuck stood up from where he was sitting on the couch. "Then let's go upstairs and get it," he said. "I want another look at that poem."

The Map

While Chuck waited in the living room, I went to retrieve the poem from my dresser. The poem was still in the top drawer hidden beneath a pile of T-shirts, just where I had left it. Beyond the fact that the poem had been given to me by the gray man, I didn't see how it held any relevance to our situation. I'd reread the poem many times over the last few months but had never been able to find any significance in the words. The poem appeared to be little more than random, meaningless lines of prose. I had no idea what new information could be gleaned by studying it further. Be that as it may, I snatched up the poem from the drawer and went to rejoin Chuck.

When I returned to the living room, I saw that Chuck was standing near the landing at the bottom of the stairs examining the Winslow Homer print hanging on the wall. I walked across the room and handed him the poem. Chuck read the poem two times and looked at the Homer print. He turned in a circle and looked all around the room. He read the poem a third time and then turned to face me.

"You know," Chuck said, "the beginning of your dream is all written down right here." He held up the poem in front of me. "I'm surprised you haven't already noticed it."

"What are you taking about?" I said. I'd read the poem at least thirty times. In my mind, the poem was nothing more than a bunch of meaningless words. What was Chuck seeing that I had missed?

I took the poem from Chuck and started reading it from the beginning. *Feel the force of life surrounds us, every fiber every strand. Don't fear for I will be here with us, conquest, conquer, living sands.*

Even though the opening line from the poem would take on great significance in the weeks to come, at the time I could see no connection whatsoever between the poem and the dream. I still didn't have a clue what Chuck was talking about. I continued reading. *Swirling mists again surround us.*

I now understood how Chuck had made the connection. There were swirling mists in the poem and swirling mists in my dream, but there was absolutely nothing in the poem about a harbor or the Winslow Homer print. I thought Chuck was really stretching his imagination and reading something into the poem that wasn't there. Chuck's smile grew deep. He moved close to me and scanned the poem with his eyes and his fingertip. The tip of his finger came to rest under the words *living sands.* He tapped on the sheet of paper and then pointed to the Homer print.

I reread the words and frowned. I looked up at the Homer print. Chuck was right. The entire poem was cryptic without question, but the words *living sands* had confounded me the most. I had puzzled and puzzled over what living sands were for many weeks. And what were we seeing in the Homer print that had so stirred our imaginations? *The ocean.* The solution to the puzzle had been literally hanging on the wall in front of me the entire time. *Living sands* were the ocean. Add the words *swirling mists* to the equation and it matched my dream perfectly. I started wondering if there was even more significance to the poem that we hadn't yet discovered.

I held the poem between Chuck and myself and we continued reading. *Forever time, time at hand* was the next line. We looked around the room, and there it was, the next piece of the puzzle: the broken cuckoo clock hanging on the wall at the bottom of the stairs. *Forever time, time at hand.* Chuck and I stepped up and onto the landing and looked at the clock. The poem was a map, and the map was leading us on a journey through my own home.

Chuck and I looked at each other knowingly and then looked down at the poem in my hand. The next line read, *Strange spaces, traces, empty faces.* I looked up at the staircase, and what I saw sent a chill down my spine. The "spaces" that made up the walls of the staircase were indeed very strange. They jutted off in weird angles and directions, but what was of even more interest were the two black-and-white profile silhouette drawings hanging on the wall along the staircase. *Strange spaces, traces, empty faces.*

I had probably looked at all of these things a thousand times, but today they were taking on a whole new meaning. Now the entire house felt electric and alive, as though the house itself was no longer made of wood and brick but was a living, breathing thing. The atmosphere around the staircase was thick with an intense, unseen energy. I took four steps up the stairs and stood in front of the silhouette drawings. I was certain that at any moment we were going to witness an extreme paranormal event.

I turned and looked down at Chuck. He was still standing at the bottom of the stairs. With my eyes I asked him, *Do I dare?* He nodded. I turned away from my friend, looked up the staircase, and read aloud the last line of the poem. *Reach now for the gifts upon the land.* I braced myself for what might come next. But nothing happened. Nothing at all. At that moment I realized that I had forgotten something. Something vital. I walked down the stairs and rejoined Chuck on the landing. He had made the same realization that I had. There was more to the poem than what was written on paper. There were still the two lines I had written in the dream.

"The next line of the poem," Chuck said. "What is it?"

I pointed to the broken cuckoo clock hanging on the wall and said, "Reset the hands, reverse the course, and then the way is clear."

"So what do we do now?" he asked.

I took in a deep breath and said, "We follow the instructions."

I reached for the clock but then hesitated. My initial reaction had been to reset the clock to 3:33, but now I thought better of it. I carefully rotated the hands counterclockwise and reset them to exactly twelve o'clock. I took four steps up the stairs and once again came to a stop next to the silhouette drawings. I folded the poem and stuck it in my back pocket. I didn't need it anymore. There was one last line to speak, and it wasn't written on any piece of paper. I stood on the staircase and spoke aloud the true last line of the poem: *Show others not your darker side, for then you must stay here.*

Chuck and I looked up at the top of the stairs, and if only for a moment, we both saw it: The familiar outline. The apparition of the gray man standing on the landing at the top of the staircase. I heard Chuck cry out, "NOOOO!" but it was too late. I was already running up the stairs.

What happened next is very difficult for me to describe to you with words because it happened so fast, but I will do my best. By the time I reached the top of the stairs, the apparition of the gray man was gone. But I had made it up there just in time to see a faint ring of blue fire on the floor as it faded into nothingness. On the perimeter where the ring of blue fire had been, I saw what I had at first mistaken to be slowly rotating shafts of light. I then realized that they weren't shafts of light, but shafts of *shadow*.

It was so cold on the landing that I could see my breath, even though my body felt very warm. The feeling of standing in the center of a powerful, unseen presence was unmistakable. I felt the familiar prickle of an electrical discharge flowing up my legs and dancing freely over my skin. I would not fully understand it until many years later, but I was standing at the edge of a portal—a portal that led to another plane of existence or possibly even another world.

I felt a sensation that can only be described as being watched by a million pairs of eyes. I could hear hundreds, perhaps thousands, of voices speaking to me inside my mind. One of the voices was louder and clearer than the others. The voice was familiar to me, and yet at the same time I was certain that I had never heard it before. Even though I couldn't understand exactly what the voice was saying to me, it was clearly the voice of a man. I knew that the man was calling out for me to join him on the other side.

I felt my own essence slowly leaving my body and drifting down into the portal. The sensation was a mixture of terror and euphoria. A part of me was afraid for my own safety, but another part of me was oddly at peace. My earlier encounters with the gray man had felt ominous and even threatening, but this time being in his presence felt more like a homecoming. It felt like the arrival of an old friend. There was a power here beyond my imagining, a power I wanted a bigger taste of. I was intoxicated by what I was experiencing. But unfortunately I wasn't the only person standing on the staircase.

I heard the sound of a loud gasp. The abruptness of the sound startled me, and my consciousness was instantly pulled back inside my body. The shadow-shafts fluxed like a mirage and vanished. I felt the portal start to close, and as this happened, the air around me grew warmer. I could no longer hear the voices or feel the intense energy flowing around me.

I turned my head and looked down at Chuck. He was still on the landing at the bottom of the stairs. The look on his face told me everything I needed to know. Chuck had seen what I had seen and felt what I had felt. His skin was a ghostly shade of white, and tears were streaming from his red eyes. The hair on his head and arms was standing straight up, and a madman's grin crossed his face. He looked exactly the way he had the night the gray man first appeared to us in the basement.

I moved to the edge of the landing and took two steps down the stairs toward him. As I did this, Chuck took two steps backward. He seemed to be afraid of me. *Why would he be afraid of me?* I wondered. I was confused and at a loss for words. I opened my arms to my friend. He took another step backward, and his back slammed hard against the wall. He just stood there for a moment, staring up at me with his wild, red eyes. Then, without speaking a word, he came rushing up the stairs and into my open arms. Chuck and I stood there on the staircase holding each other, laughing and crying at what we had experienced.

For the longest time, Chuck and I sat together in the living room in complete silence. Even though the experience was still fresh, my memories of it were quickly growing distant, like the memories of my early childhood. It felt like I was having to reach across many years of time to access them. As I sat there on the couch, I realized that the horn had only been a catalyst—a catalyst that, for lack of better words, had activated the poem. Or to be precise, it had activated our minds, allowing us to discover what the poem really was.

In reality, the poem had been a map. A map that had led us directly to the gray man. The entire thing had been planned from the very beginning. The gray man had given me the poem. He had given me the dream and haunted me with the horn, which in turn had caused us to investigate the poem. Our investigation had taken us on a journey that led directly to the source. It had led us back to the gray man. A man, I knew, that wasn't really a man at all, but something else. Something impossible. We had been manipulated by an entity that possessed not only intelligence, but wisdom.

None of what we had seen and experienced over the past few months had been random. None of it had been a coincidence. The poem and the dream, the horn and the numbers, the materializations and even the malfunctioning stereo system were as one. Every bit of it was interrelated and was designed to guide us in a very specific direction. And the scariest part of all was that everything appeared to be linked directly back to *us*. Everything was linked to the members of a simple rock 'n' roll band named Entropy. The five of us were inescapably bound to an entity from another world.

Chuck and I went on to discuss many things that night, and among them was this apparent connection to the gray man. In the end, we decided that it was in our best interest to fill the rest of the guys in on what we had experienced and what we believed to be true. Whether they liked it or not, our bandmates were as connected to the gray man as Chuck and I were. In our minds, there was no question about it. The unanswered question was whether or not the five of us would eventually become allied with the entity or imprisoned by it.

When I finally asked Chuck why he had reacted with fear when I had approached him on the stairs, he was hesitant to speak about it. When he finally opened up, I knew he wasn't telling me the whole story. I knew there were things he had felt and seen that he was holding back from me. But what he eventually did tell me is that he had been frightened because he had seen *two* of me standing at the top of the stairs that day and that my eyes had turned pitch black.

Before Chuck went home for the evening, he asked me if I needed him to stay the night. He was concerned that after our fresh encounter with the gray man, I might be afraid to spend the night in the house alone. I thanked Chuck for his offer but told him I would be just fine. What I didn't tell him is that there was something I needed to do that would have been impossible to accomplish with another person in the house. I knew that if I was going to move forward, I had to conquer my fear of the unknown.

That night I summoned every bit of courage I had left in me. I went to the living room and unplugged the clock radio from the wall. I walked upstairs to the guest room, set the clock on the vanity, and plugged it in. Then I pulled back the covers and crawled into bed.

I awoke the next morning feeling more rested and alive than I had in a very long time. I had slept straight through the entire night without once being disturbed. No dream. No horn. No glowing handprints or unexplainable shadows on the wall. That night I had shed my fear of sleeping alone in the guest room. I had conquered my fear of the unknown. After that night, I was never again awakened by the dream or the sound of the horn blasting in my ear.

Later that same morning, Chuck and the rest of the guys showed up at my place unannounced. Chuck had taken it upon himself to inform our bandmates of the incidents of the previous day. He had also told them about the horn, my dream, the map, and the numbers on the clock. He had even told them about the shadow and the glowing handprints Shelby and I had seen in the guest room weeks earlier.

I didn't have a problem with the fact that Chuck had told the guys these things, but on the other hand, I really didn't expect that they would believe a single word of it. But once again, I was wrong. As it turned out, Trice, Jeff, and L.B. had all been having strange dreams of their own and had been seeing sequential numbers on clocks on a regular basis. The strangeness that had engulfed my entire existence had spread to my bandmates like a supernatural virus.

That day, the five of us made a unanimous decision that would alter the course of our lives and the direction of the band. We made the decision to stop living in fear of the gray man and the power he possessed. We instead decided to run toward that power and use it to our advantage. We were all very excited about the potential that appeared to be within our grasp. And who could have blamed us? This was the rarest of opportunities imaginable. After all, how many rock 'n' roll bands on the planet had an otherworldly force to guide them?

Yes, it was an exciting time, without question, but I couldn't shake the feeling that gaining the favor of the gray man had come at a terrible price. The truth was that our footsteps were being haunted by something far older, wiser, and more manipulative than we ever could have imagined.

CHRONICLE THREE
The Force

The Becoming
March 1981

The day I turned twenty-one years old, everything appeared to be going my way. But as the saying goes, appearances can be deceiving.

Six months had passed since Chuck and I had discovered the map and encountered the gray man on the stairs. We were still just kids in those days, barely out of our teens, and we had been enlisted by an otherworldly entity for a reason we didn't fully understand. In our naivety, the five of us had embraced the power that had come into our lives, and we guarded it with a jealous ferocity. We had bonded with this power and the near-constant presence of the gray man. But now we were no longer referring to the entity as the "gray man." Now we commonly referred to the entity and its power as The Force. This had absolutely nothing to do with the *Star Wars* movies, even though we were all big fans (and who wasn't in those days?), but rather the opening line from the poem: *Feel the force of life surrounds us.*

We had welcomed The Force into our lives without fear of consequence. We did this because the five of us had agreed that we couldn't allow our own fear to control us. Even though we were very young men and didn't have the advantage of decades of life experience, we had an abundance of street smarts. We knew that given the right environment, a single seed of fear can grow into something much more powerful and dangerous than the thing that gave birth to it.

The entity, the power that we called The Force was no figment of our imagination, nor was it a mere poltergeist or ghost. Whatever The Force really was, it was powerful. It was capable of manipulating people and objects on our plane of existence as it saw fit. We fell in love with this newfound power. We had blindly accepted The Force into our lives, but despite our confidence (or perhaps because of it), we had no real control over it whatsoever.

For the members of Entropy, being in the presence of The Force had become commonplace. We wrapped ourselves in the very fabric of The Force and wore it like armor. We started believing that we were invincible. We were certain that The Force was guiding the five of us to fame and fortune. Every signal we received from the entity seemed to reinforce this conviction.

The five members of Entropy were now seeing sequential numbers on such a regular basis that they were a part of our everyday lives. We used The Force as a supernatural compass to guide us in the right direction. When we made good or bad decisions about our own futures or the direction of the band, The Force would speak to us through numbers on the clock. My number was 3:33, and Jeff's was 2:22. For Chuck it was 5:55. Trice's number was 4:44, and L.B.'s was 1:11.

When The Force was trying to get our attention or lead us in a specific direction, we would see sequential numbers on the clock for days or even weeks at a time. When we learned the lessons we needed to learn or had made the right decisions, The Force would inform us of this by repeatedly showing us numbers on the clock that were off by a single digit, such as 3:34 or 1:12. The numbers would always be one digit clockwise (5:56), never counterclockwise (1:10). In a rudimentary way, we had established a form of diplomacy with The Force and had learned how to speak its language. But although this form of communication was consistent, it wasn't very efficient. And looking back on it now, I realize that the scariest part was that all this was starting to feel normal.

The presence of The Force now held sway over every aspect of Entropy. Nowhere was its influence more apparent than in our music. Our music and lyrics began to exhibit a powerful, otherworldly quality that in many ways mirrored the unearthly aspect of The Force itself. Jeff started journaling about the band in a book he called *Until Entropy: A Focus.*

I, in turn, compiled the band's lyrics into a hardbound volume that I simply titled *Entropy*. Returning to my roots in the visual arts, I started drawing complex pieces of artwork to accompany the sheets of lyrics we had written. These drawings reflected the root meanings of the lyrics and their never-ending connection to the gray man. I would paste the drawings in my book adjacent to the appropriate lyrics. Upon occasion I would even incorporate lines of lyrics into the drawings themselves. I was pleased with the artwork I had created, but the one thing that had eluded my artistic creativity was the perfect logo for the band.

One day while I was flipping through the pages of a leftover textbook from one of my high school art classes, a rather interesting and unique illustration caught my eye. It was an illustration of a Penrose triangle.

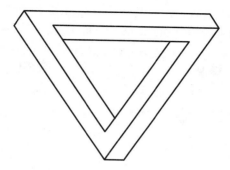

The Penrose triangle, also know as the Penrose tribar or the "impossible triangle," is an optical illusion that was created by Swedish artist Oscar Reutersvärd in 1834. I was fascinated with the triangle not only because of its peculiarity, but also because, not unlike our friend the gray man, the Penrose triangle was an object that cannot possibly exist in three-dimensional space.

I adopted the Penrose triangle for Entropy and incorporated it as an essential and symbolic part of the band's logo. The Penrose triangle became so well loved by the band, in fact, that the guys insisted that I learn how to paint with an airbrush so I could create my own renditions of the triangle that were consistent with the artwork of the time period. Prompted by the guys' requests, I eventually did learn how to paint with an airbrush, and the symbol of the Penrose triangle soon adorned the heads of L.B.'s bass drums, the fronts of our guitars, and pretty much everything else I could get my hands on.

Entropy and The Force were now synonymous in a way that no one outside of the five of us could truly understand. Or, to be more precise, we were synonymous in a way that no one outside the seven of us could truly understand. And exactly what do I mean by saying the seven of us? The five members of Entropy believed that when we aligned ourselves with the gray man, we had in essence added a sixth member to the band. We further believed that once the six of us were combined into a single unit, we collectively created a seventh entity that we called The Force. Evidence of this belief can be found in the opening line of the poem that had been given to me by the gray man: *Feel the force of life surrounds us, every fiber, every strand.*

You may recall that I mentioned previously that the beginning of the poem seemingly had no connection to my dream, or to anything else we had been experiencing for that matter. You may also recall that in that chapter I told you that the beginning of the poem would take on great significance in the months to come. To unravel the mystery of "seven," let's take another look at the beginning of the poem.

Feel the force of life surrounds us, every fiber, every strand. Don't fear for I will be here with us, conquest conquer, living sands. The line of the poem we need to examine is *Don't fear for I will be here with us.* In this line, the entity (represented by the word I) speaks of itself as being an entity distinctly separate from itself, and yet is still a part of the whole (us) that is the sum of Entropy and the entity combined into a single unit. In other words, when the gray man and the five members of Entropy aligned, we became six, but the pooled resources of the six of us combined to create a seventh entity we called The Force.

The importance of seven was further revealed in our writings and in our music. Jeff became so obsessed with the concept that he devoted an entire chapter of musings on seven (or "seveign," as he spelled it) in his book. The rest of us took liberties with Jeff's colorful use of spelling and playfully augmented it by writing a song we called "Old Number Seveign." This song was not only a play on Jeff's spelling, but also a play on the Jack Daniel's brand of Tennessee whiskey (which, by no coincidence, was Chuck's all-time favorite adult beverage), which features the words "Old No. 7 Brand" on its label. The song "Old Number Seveign" was almost entirely instrumental and concluded with L.B. playing a fifteen-minute drum solo.

Without question, "Old Number Seveign" was one of our favorite songs. The song also gave Chuck, Trice, and me the chance to sit down with Jeff for a few minutes during our rehearsals and fully enjoy L.B.'s considerable drum skills. In a word, "Old Number Seveign" was a joy. But in the not-so-distant future, that song would evoke a very different emotion.

That same year, Chuck's mother passed away, and she bequeathed him a considerable inheritance. Chuck promptly sank a good chunk of that money into the band in the form of microphones and a brand-new sound system. He also used some of the money to buy himself a gorgeous Gibson Les Paul guitar. And lastly, Chuck used some of the money to book the band into a local recording studio so we could record a proper demo of our music.

We took full advantage of the opportunity to record a demo, and before going into the studio, we set the poem to music, something we'd been meaning to do for quite some time. As it turned out, that song (which for obvious reasons we titled "The Force") became one of our best pieces of original music. The recording process went seamlessly, and we left the studio with a wonderful four-song demo tape in our hands, even though during the process the sound engineer had commented several times that he was confused as to why his tape counter was constantly resetting itself to 333.

The demo tape and new sound system allowed Entropy to book more gigs. In the past we had struggled with booking shows, but given the time period and the local musical environment, that wasn't surprising in the least. Entropy's set list was composed solely of original material, something that was practically unheard of in northern Colorado in those days. At the time, very few area bands wrote and performed original music. And the bands that did write originals were lucky to get away with slipping one or two of their own songs into set lists that mostly comprised cover songs. The majority of those original songs didn't go over very well with local audiences.

As a result of the local music scene and our short, original set list, Entropy was resigned to opening for cover bands at nightclubs and playing at parties. Our music was incredibly well accepted given the circumstances, but we still hadn't been able to book a breakthrough gig that would get us noticed by promoters and larger venues. But unlike any other band in Colorado, and possibly even in the entire world, we had an ally on our side the likes of which had never before been seen. The power of The Force refused to be contained.

One night while Trice and I were in the basement working on the music and lyrics for a new song, we received an unexpected visitor. Upon answering the knock on my front door, I discovered that the visitor was a rotund man named Jack Foreman. Jack appeared to be in his early thirties, was sporting an enormous beard and a ponytail, and had a dark green folder tucked under his right arm. And judging by the clothing and patch-covered leather vest he was wearing, Jack was a biker.

After I invited Jack inside and introduced him to Trice, the large man informed us that a good friend of his had heard Entropy play at a party and had been very impressed with our music. Jack further informed us that he was in charge of booking and promoting the entertainment for a huge outdoor festival that was scheduled to take place in Colorado Springs in early June. Much to our surprise and delight, Jack told us that he was very interested in the possibility of adding Entropy to the lineup of musical acts he had already scheduled for the event.

After listening to our demo tape and a few impromptu jams Trice and I threw together on the spot, Jack was sold. A few beers and some considerable chattering later, Jack told us he had a long ride back to his home in Niwot, Colorado, and that he needed to get on the road. He handed me a contract that was tucked away inside the folder he was carrying and told us to get back to him after we discussed the gig with the rest of the guys.

Trice and I followed Jack up the stairs, out the front door, and onto the porch, completely expecting to see a fully dressed Harley Davidson motorcycle parked in the driveway. And we weren't disappointed. After thoroughly checking out Jack's motorcycle (a stunning 1970 FL 1200 Electra Glide), drooling over all the chrome, and expressing our envy, we said goodbye to Jack as he mounted his bike. With a thunderous roar and a salute, he disappeared into the night.

After returning to the basement and looking over the contract Jack had given us, Trice and I made a discovery that was as enticing as it was terrifying. According to the language of the contract, the festival was a four-day event and was expected to draw between two and three thousand attendees at any given time. The contract also stated that for a single performance the band would be paid five hundred dollars in cash.

We were stunned, not by the money (we estimated that five hundred dollars would be just enough to cover our expenses) but by the expected size of the audience. The largest audience Entropy had ever played for was somewhere around three hundred people. The festival organizers were predicting about three times that number. I wondered if we were ready to play for such a large crowd, but I knew that my wondering was pointless. There was no way in hell we could allow such an opportunity to slip between our fingers. Ready or not, Entropy had finally booked a monster of a gig.

On with the Show
June 1981

It was warm for early June in the rain shadow of the Rocky Mountains, and as we packed our gear in our vehicles and prepared to make the 150-mile drive to Colorado Springs, we were as nervous as we were excited about the upcoming show. We were also starting to get a little worried. Chuck was two hours overdue, and we had no idea what could be keeping him. Over the last hour I'd made three attempts to reach him by phone but couldn't get an answer. Wherever Chuck was, he obviously wasn't at home.

Shelby and Janice were planning to attend the festival but had made the decision to drive to Colorado Springs on their own. That was a good thing considering Entropy's collective vehicles were already crammed full of gear, clothing, and personal items. As Jeff was helping L.B. load the last of his drum kit into the back of his pickup truck, Chuck finally pulled into my driveway.

As Chuck brought his car to a stop and killed the engine, I approached the vehicle. He noticed me coming and rolled down the driver's side window. I immediately started giving him hell for being so late. Chuck just smiled up at me, opened the door, and climbed out of the car. To no one's surprise, he was dressed in black from head to toe.

Chuck apologized for worrying me and said he had a few surprises for the band that had taken him longer to gather than he had anticipated. He stepped to the rear of the car and unlocked the trunk. I followed him back there, and my eyes beheld an aspiring keyboardist's wet dream. Nestled inside the trunk was a Korg Trident analog synthesizer in all its electronic glory. Chuck was quick to point out that the synthesizer was only a rental unit for the gig, but he told me that if I liked it, he'd do what he could to help me purchase one of my very own.

Even though the Korg was only a temporary fixture, I was thrilled to have it for the show. The sole synthesizer I owned was only capable of producing a small variety of sounds and was little more than an overpriced toy. The Korg was a professional, top-of-the-line instrument.

As excited as I was about the Korg, I was also terrified of it. The keyboard parts I played in our songs were minimal and little more than ear candy, but the bottom line was that I had never even seen a Korg Trident before, let alone played one. I didn't have the slightest clue how the damn thing worked. After expressing my fears about the synthesizer to Chuck, he soothed me by saying that he'd had the presence of mind to ask for the owner's manual when he rented it. He assured me that I would have plenty of time to study the manual during the drive. He also informed me that the Korg had a headphone jack and that I would undoubtedly have some time to play around with it backstage before the show. I agreed with Chuck's reasoning and leaned over the trunk to get a better look at the Korg's menagerie of knobs and switches. But as I did this, something sitting in the trunk next to the synthesizer caught my attention.

From the time he was a sophomore in high school, Chuck had been taking lessons in the martial arts. Taekwondo, to be precise. Neatly folded and lying in the trunk next to the Korg were two martial arts uniforms, also known as gi. Nested inside the uniforms were two black belts. This was Chuck's second surprise. After years of training, he had finally attained a first-degree black belt in taekwondo.

I assumed that Chuck had brought along the uniforms and belts to show them off to the guys and me, but as it turned out, he had something entirely different in mind for the uniforms. He wanted Trice and me to wear them at the show. Upon hearing Chuck's plan, I flatly refused. I made the argument that Trice and I had no training in martial arts whatsoever, and that to have us wear the uniforms onstage, the black belts in particular—belts that we hadn't earned—would be outrageous and disrespectful.

Chuck countered my argument by saying that he thought the uniforms would look really cool onstage and that he had no intention of allowing us to wear the black belts as part of the getup. He told me that he had also brought along the two white belts that originally came with the uniforms. Chuck figured that the white belts would be okay for us to wear because they signified that the wearer had no training whatsoever. I told Chuck that I would talk things over with Trice but that the uniforms would probably make us look like two half-assed Jedi knights. For the time being I was making no promises.

While Chuck went to check on the other guys and help them load up the last of the equipment, I went into the house and called Shelby to find out what time they were planning on hitting the road. Shelby told me that they still had to run a few errands for Janice's mother and that they'd probably be a few hours behind us. She said that they would just hunt us down at the festival. A half hour later, our musical caravan was on the road and headed for Colorado Springs.

As we pulled up to the festival gates, the atmosphere was magical and alive. The festival was taking place on many acres of private land, and the seclusion of the property had cast its spell on everyone attending. Lining both sides of the dirt roads that extended throughout the grounds were hundreds upon hundreds of motorcycles, cars, and pickup trucks. The diversity of the crowd was amazing to behold. Mixed in with an untold number of bikers we saw everything from cowboys to hippies, rednecks to jocks. Beautiful women, young and old, were wandering everywhere. And much to our pleasure, some of them were topless.

It was a Saturday afternoon, the last day of the festival, and the attendees were making the most of it. The smells of barbeque and weed filled the air, and beer and liquor were flowing like water. There were rows of vendors selling their wares and a gaming area where people were tossing horseshoes and yard darts. The sounds of laughter and music and the roar of motorcycles were all around us.

In the distance, we could see the stage we would be playing on later in the evening. The stage was enormous, easily three times larger than any stage we had ever performed on. High above the main platform I could see a framework of metal scaffolding lined with stage lighting. On either side of the stage were towering columns of speakers, and floating in the air above each of the columns was a helium balloon in the shape of a blimp. Sitting on the front of the stage were footlights and pro-grade sound monitors. It was obvious that whoever had set up the stage knew exactly what they were doing.

After we spoke with the guards at the gate and told them who we were, they directed us to a side road that led behind the stage and to the place where we were supposed to unload and store our equipment. As we slowly drove along, I noticed that my bandmates were doing a considerable amount of rubbernecking. I was guilty of a little rubbernecking myself. But who could have blamed us? There was an incredible party going on, and we were eager to get our gear unloaded and do some mingling.

As we pulled around to the back of the stage, two men from security greeted us. They were without a doubt the largest men I had ever seen. They were so huge, in fact, that upon laying eyes on them, I was certain they'd missed their life's calling and could have easily had brilliant careers playing defense for the Denver Broncos. After they showed us where to unload our equipment, I asked the large men if they knew where I could find Jack Foreman. I wanted to find out what time slot we would be playing in. I was told that Jack had been running around all day like a chicken with its head chopped off and that I should just check back from time to time. I was assured that Jack would find his way back to the stage eventually.

After our equipment was unloaded and secured, the five of us wandered into the crowd to do a little sightseeing. It was a glorious day, the kind of day that makes a person glad to be alive, and we were as happy as we could possibly be. But sadly, a black cloud was about to appear on the horizon. A cloud in the shape of an old friend.

As the five of us were wandering the grounds, we were delighted to see a familiar face. It was the face of one of our oldest and closest friends, Tom Willson. We hadn't heard from Tom in months and were pleased to see that he had heard about the festival and had decided to attend.

Upon walking up to greet our friend, we could instantly tell that something was very wrong. Tom looked frail and had lost a considerable amount of weight. Tom had always been outgoing and strong-willed. He was the kind of man who inspired others to do the very best they could. But now, Tom's presence felt murky and dark, nearly lifeless. We soon discovered that Tom was suffering from a disease rarely found in men. Tom had been diagnosed with male breast cancer and had been told by his doctors that he didn't have long to live. As unfathomable as it was, our friend, a man still in his early twenties, was dying.

We spent the next hour talking to Tom and doing our best to console him, even though it was obvious that our words were hollow and meaningless. We stayed with Tom as long as we could, but I soon noticed that there was activity taking place on the stage. I could see a group of men up there setting up band equipment. As terrible as I felt about leaving, I simply had to get back to the stage to see if I could locate Jack Foreman. Chuck, Jeff, and L.B. stayed with Tom a while longer, but Trice and I excused ourselves and headed back to the stage. Along the way we kept a sharp eye out for Shelby and Janice, but the girls were nowhere to be found. We were starting to get more than a little concerned as to their whereabouts.

As Trice and I neared the stage, we finally spotted Jack Foreman. As foretold, he was backstage running around like the proverbial chicken with its head chopped off. Jack greeted us with a big smile and a handshake, and before we could get the words out of our mouths to ask, he informed us that we would be performing second, around two and a half hours later.

I calculated that Jack's estimate would put Entropy onstage just around dusk. This was welcome news. By dusk, the heat of the day would be starting to pass and the stage lighting would look simply spectacular. The evening's headliner, a popular local band called Double Jeopardy, would follow Entropy's performance and conclude the musical portion of the festival.

Running short on time, Trice and I headed around the back of the stage to where our equipment was being stored. I still hadn't taken the time to check out the Korg synthesizer, and if I was intending on using it during our performance, this was a must. I located a pair of headphones in one of our storage bins and found an unused outlet where I plugged in the Korg. While I was learning how to use the synthesizer, Trice made his way onstage and started chatting up members of the opening act.

Around thirty minutes later, the opening act (whose name I cannot recall) took the stage in full rock 'n' roll regalia. The act was a cover band with a southern flair, and their set list consisted of songs by popular major acts of the day such as Molly Hatchet, 38 Special, and George Thorogood and the Destroyers. The opening act sounded decent and was reasonably well accepted by the audience, but all in all they offered little more than what a person might expect to hear from an average local bar band.

About halfway through their performance, the rest of the guys joined Trice and me backstage and started assembling their gear. Even though the festival coordinators had provided plenty of stagehands, we needed to make sure our equipment was ready to go at a moment's notice. We wanted to make a seamless transition during the intermission.

Just as L.B. was seeing to the last details of assembling his drum set, we received some unsettling news from Jack Foreman. Jack informed us that the lead singer for Double Jeopardy had taken ill and had requested a major change in the lineup. Double Jeopardy's singer was feeling worse by the minute and that the band had requested to play next. This changeup meant that we would close the show.

This was terrific news. But it was also terrible news. The change in the lineup meant that Entropy would take on the role of surrogate headliner. The problem with this arrangement was that, with few exceptions, the members of the ever-growing audience had never even heard the name of our band before, let alone our music. The members of Double Jeopardy were local musical heroes. We were virtual unknowns. As far as the audience was concerned, we might as well have been aliens from another world. Playing last carried the very real risk that we might be booed off the stage. But we had little choice in the matter. To refuse would have been extremely rude to the members of Double Jeopardy and would have put us in a bad light with the promoters. There was no way around it: Entropy was going to close the show.

Just as the sun was setting behind the mountains, Double Jeopardy took the stage in front of a rowdy sea of fans. By my estimation, there were well over two thousand people in the audience and somewhere around that same number scattered throughout the festival grounds. The band started out with a strong cover of Led Zeppelin's "Dazed and Confused," but halfway into their third number, it was obvious to everyone that the band's lead singer wasn't feeling well. The singer had started the show vibrant and animated, but now he was listless and his vocals were growing weaker by the minute.

Halfway through Double Jeopardy's set, we were informed by Jack that the band would be leaving the stage after just one more song. Our already difficult situation had just gotten worse. Double Jeopardy's early exit meant that we would have to fill the space left vacant by their short performance. This meant that we would be forced to play new and untested material in front of an unfamiliar audience.

As Double Jeopardy finished up their performance, we scurried around backstage making final preparations to take the stage. Shelby and Janice were still missing in action, and Trice and I were more nervous than ever. We had no idea where our girlfriends could be. After a quick consult with Trice, the two of us decided to don the martial arts uniforms Chuck had brought along for us. We were uncertain how the uniforms would go over with the crowd, but there was no point in playing things safe now. The uniforms were lightweight versions and were quite comfortable to wear. In a way that neither Trice nor I could explain, the uniforms bolstered our confidence, even though the guys from security jokingly told us that the uniforms would probably prompt a few members of the audience to try to kick our asses. At least we hoped they were joking.

On their way off the stage, the members of Double Jeopardy took a moment to thank us for our help. Understandably, their lead singer in particular seemed genuinely grateful. With Jeff's help and direction, the stagehands had our equipment set up in no time flat. After our gear was powered up and checked, Jeff gave us the thumbs up. It was show time.

I strapped my guitar across my shoulder and, with my bandmates behind me, headed for the center of the stage. I felt the familiar euphoria and butterflies fluttering around in my stomach as I stepped up to the microphone and announced the name of the band. A few immediate calls for songs by Lynyrd Skynyrd and Bruce Springsteen sounded from somewhere in the audience. Such requests were hardly unusual, but given the circumstances, they were making us more nervous than ever. Entropy played no cover songs whatsoever, and our originals were entirely unknown to this rural audience. The crowd was more boisterous than ever, and I had no idea what to expect.

Bathed in the glare of footlights, I turned my head and gave L.B. a nod. The sound of his drumsticks clacking together four times reverberated through the night, and we broke into our first song. The music booming from the loudspeakers sounded incredible and was mixed to perfection. The song we had chosen to open with was "The Force." Four bars into the intro of the song I was to play my first notes on the new synthesizer. In my haste, I had only skimmed over the user manual. This oversight was about to run up and bite me in the ass.

I stepped up to the Korg and positioned my hands on the keys. The synthesizer parts I had written for our opening number not only sounded great but were the very definition of simplicity. All I had to manage was a soaring, siren-like run followed by a repeating four-note pattern. I looked out into the audience with a huge smile on my face and pressed down on the keys. What came blasting from the loudspeakers should have been the ethereal battle cry of an archangel. What came out instead was the sound of a cat being hacked to death with an axe.

Chuck and Trice jerked their heads and looked in my direction. Even though he was behind me and I couldn't see him, I could feel L.B.'s eyes burning a hole in the back of my head. The look in Trice's eyes was asking me, *What the fuck just happened?* In a word, I had just happened. While studying the user manual, I had overlooked one very important detail. Unlike any synthesizer or keyboard I had ever played before, the Korg had to be tuned similar to the way a guitar had to be tuned. There was even a big, shiny knob on the face of the Korg to accomplish this task. In my rush to get our equipment onstage, I had missed this. The Korg wasn't even close to being in tune with the rest of the band. We'd had one shot to make a great first impression on this audience, and I had ruined it. I had made the biggest amateur mistake of all time and fucked up everything. Or so I had thought.

After the failed note, the next sound I expected to hear was a chorus of boos rising from the crowd. But that sound never came. What I heard instead was the sound of tremendous cheering. Despite the sour note, the audience loved what they were hearing. I quickly righted my mistake and got the Korg in tune with the band. Entropy powered our way through the rest of the song and ended it to another round of cheers. We got through our next song without incident, but by the time we started playing our third song, I noticed that something very strange was happening to the audience. Our music was affecting the audience like a siren's song. Only minutes earlier, the crowd had been raucous and on the verge of getting out of control. But now they were spellbound. Even I was spellbound by what I was experiencing.

In many ways, being onstage and performing for this audience was no different than what I had experienced the day Chuck and I had discovered the map and the portal at the top of the stairs. The glare from the lights flooding the stage made it almost impossible to see anything in front of me. I could hear the voices of the fans and feel their presence, but beyond that, little else. The world beyond the stage and the audience became something intangible. The world's billions of inhabitants became ghostlike and no longer mattered. All that mattered was the moment. The sound of L.B.'s drums felt ancient and tribal, and it charged the atmosphere with its primitive energy. I felt more like a shaman leading a ritual than a rock musician performing for an audience. I could feel the presence of The Force flowing all around me. The sensation was as unmistakable as it was beautiful.

But a moment later, these intensely beautiful feelings were replaced by a very different emotion. At least they were replaced for Trice and me. As Trice and I were standing onstage, we felt what could only be described as a ripple in the energy surrounding us followed by an overwhelming feeling of doom. The feeling came without warning and was centered on Shelby and Janice. Something very bad had happened to our girlfriends. We were certain of it. Neither the audience nor the rest of the guys in the band seemed to have felt this disturbance, but for Trice and me the ominous feeling was unmistakable. We just stood there in the center of the stage, playing our instruments and staring at each other with very worried looks on our faces. Without speaking a word Trice and I were having one of the most important conversations of our lives. But we were also putting on the show of our lives. Despite our worries, we had no choice but to play on.

An hour and half later, we were nearing the end of our performance, and there was a single song remaining on our set list. The song was "Old Number Seveign." The audience loved the song, and L.B.'s drum solo was stronger than ever. We had dominated the stage, and our show ended with a tremendous surge of musical prowess. As we thanked the audience and exited the stage, demands for an encore were sounding everywhere in the crowd. But even though we desperately wanted to play another song, we never retook the stage. When we began our performance, the last thing we'd expected were calls for an encore, and we didn't have a single song left in reserve. We'd given the audience everything we had.

Not wanting to repeat ourselves or play an impromptu jam, we decided it was best to leave things where they stood and call it a night. We had managed to overcome extreme adversity, and that was good enough for us. As we retreated backstage and unstrapped our guitars, Trice and I were treated to a very welcome sight.

Standing backstage and talking to the security guards were Shelby and Janice. Our girlfriends had an alarming tale to tell. The girls told us they'd been in a terrible car accident just outside the city limits of Colorado Springs— an accident that no one could explain, not even the police. According to Shelby and Janice, as they were nearing the city limits and passing through an intersection, a Ford pickup truck had run a red light and come very close to hitting them. The girls told us the truck would have T-boned them at a high rate of speed and they probably would have been killed if something unexplainable hadn't happened.

They told us that just before the truck would have crashed into the side of the car, something had prevented the accident from taking place.

Janice told us that everything had happened so quickly that she hadn't had time to apply the brakes or attempt to steer clear of the truck. She told us that a split second before the truck would have hit them, an unseen force pulled her car out of the intersection and onto the shoulder of the road. The girls told us that as this was happening, they felt the front of the car being lifted up and off the road, "like a giant, invisible hand had grabbed on to the front of the car and pulled us out of the way of the truck," Janice told us.

As unbelievable as their story was, Janice had a police report to back up her account of what had happened. Even though the truck never hit them, there was extensive damage to the front of Janice's car—damage that not even the police could explain. Janice motioned for Trice and me to follow her, and we went to have a look at the vehicle.

As we approached Janice's car (a silver 1977 Toyota Corolla), the damage was obvious even from thirty yards away. Just as Janice had described, it looked like a gigantic hand had grabbed on to the front of her car and crushed it like an aluminum can. The hood, bumper, and both front quarter panels of her car were caved in, yet the paint was still intact. Another implausible fact was that the damage was mostly cosmetic and hadn't rendered the car undrivable. It was unlike any vehicular damage I had ever seen. According to the girls and the police report, even though the driver of the Ford pickup admitted to running the red light, his vehicle never came into contact with Janice's car. Nor did anything else, for that matter—at least nothing that could be seen with human eyes. There was no rational explanation for the damage to Janice's car.

Neither the police nor our girlfriends could explain the damage or the averted accident, but Trice and I certainly could. Even though Trice and I never spoke a word to the girls about what we knew to be true, an entity from another plane of existence had prevented the accident from taking place. The gray man had intervened and shielded the girls from harm. The unexplainable damage to the car alone was enough evidence to convince even a nonbeliever of this truth. And not only were Trice and I believers, we were an inseparable part of the very force that had done the deed. After examining the vehicle from front to back, the four of us walked away from the car and rejoined the rest of Entropy behind the stage.

After Trice and I loaded our equipment into our cars, we took Shelby and Janice for a walk through the festival in hopes of cheering them up. Our plan took root, and before long the girls started acting like their normal selves. As we made our way through the crowd, Trice and I were showered with words of praise for our performance from many a passerby. The girls expressed their displeasure at missing most of the show, but unbeknownst to us, they had arrived at the festival in time to hear us play our last two songs from backstage.

As we walked along, we ran into Tom Willson for a second time. Tom looked much happier than he had earlier in the day when he had told us the bad news about his health. In fact, our friend looked downright elated. Tom explained that he had spent the last hour or so talking to a young black man who had claimed to be a very close friend of the band. This man was responsible for raising Tom's spirits. Entropy had quite a few African American fans and acquaintances, but no one who could have been considered a close friend.

I was quite interested in finding out more about this person. I was just about to ask Tom for the man's name when Jeff came running up behind us through the crowd. He was calling out to us at the top of his voice. As we turned to face Jeff, we could see that he was panicked and on the verge of tears. After taking a few seconds to catch his breath, Jeff told us that some very valuable pieces of the band's equipment had been stolen from one of our cars.

As we came running up to where the cars were parked, I saw that Chuck was pacing in front of L.B.'s pickup truck and talking to Jack Foreman. Once we were within earshot, I heard that a bin containing every single microphone Entropy owned was missing from the back of the truck, the very same microphones that Chuck had recently purchased for the band with his own money. Also missing from the back of truck were both of Chuck's guitars. Chuck's Gibson Les Paul was a recent addition and could be repurchased at any well-stocked music store, but the other guitar that had been stolen was the Ibanez Iceman that Chuck had owned since he was a sophomore in high school. The Iceman was Chuck's very first guitar and was irreplaceable.

The theft was a terrible misfortune for everyone concerned, but Jeff in particular was livid and beside himself with shame. It was Jeff's job to watch over the vehicles to make sure something like this didn't happen, and he had failed at that job. Jeff had abandoned his post for only a few moments, but it was enough time to give the thief (or thieves) the opportunity to make off with our gear. The cars had been parked reasonably close to the rear of the stage, and Jack Foreman and the security guards were also unhappy with themselves for not witnessing the crime. Be that as it may, our gear was gone and there was little hope of getting it back. A thief with even half a brain would be long gone by now. The culprit had made a clean getaway with the equipment.

Jack extended the possibility that the landowner's insurance provider might cover the loss, and I in turn pointed out it was possible that L.B.'s car insurance might pay replacement costs for the stolen items. But even with the possibility of recouping the loss by way of insurance, Jack felt terrible about what had happened. He graciously offered to pay us two hundred and fifty dollars more than we had been con-tracted for to help pay for the stolen gear.

Jack told us he wished he could pay every penny of what the equipment was worth, but that this was the first year of the festival and that due to startup costs the event had lost a considerable amount of money. The extra two hundred and fifty dollars Jack had offered would be com-ing out of his own pocket. And it was for that reason alone that Chuck declined to take the money. All of the stolen equipment belonged to him anyway, so it was his call to make. Chuck thanked Jack for his generous offer but told him we would figure out a way to cover the costs on our own.

With conflicted hearts, we bid Jack and his crew fare-well, climbed into our vehicles, and made the long drive back home.

A week after the theft, Chuck placed an ad in the *Colorado Springs Gazette* offering a fifteen-hundred-dollar reward for the return of his equipment. After placing the ad, Chuck received a phone call from a man claiming that he had been hired to act as a middleman in negotiating the return of the equipment for the reward money. Chuck arranged to meet with this man north of Colorado Springs in a town called Castle Rock. The arrangement called for Chuck to show the middleman the money and for the middleman to show Chuck at least one piece of the stolen equipment. If both sides were satisfied, the middleman would collect the remainder of the equipment from the thief and exchange it for the cash. If everything went as planned, Chuck would get all of his equipment back at one third of the replacement cost.

There was, however, a little problem with this plan. Chuck didn't have all of the reward money. After telling us about the ad and the arrangement he had made, Chuck confessed that he had blown through his entire inheritance and was broke. The only money he could spare toward the reward amounted to less than three hundred dollars. Upon hearing of his dilemma, Trice and I offered to sell our backup guitars to cover the shortage, but Chuck refused to take our money.

In fact, we soon discovered that Chuck had no intention of paying the entire reward. Chuck's plan was to meet with the middleman as had been arranged and show him a large roll of bills. His idea was to place a single hundred-dollar bill on the outside of the roll and to pad the center with ones. Chuck planned to show the middleman this roll of bills during their initial meeting. If Chuck's ruse worked and the middleman returned with the rest of the gear, Chuck would confess that he didn't have all the money. If the middleman wasn't okay with that, Chuck planned to take possession of his equipment anyway, and if necessary by force.

Chuck's plan was a dangerous proposition, but the members of Entropy were fiercely loyal to one another. We told Chuck that we would go to Castle Rock with him, and that if it came down to a fight, we had his back. But Chuck flatly refused our assistance. He told us that he planned to meet with the middleman alone.

After a long argument about the recklessness of his plan, Chuck finally agreed to allow a single member of Entropy to accompany him to Castle Rock. The member he chose was L.B. The rest of us weren't very happy with this arrangement, but the decision had been made, and changing Chuck's mind simply wasn't possible. The next morning as Chuck and L.B. backed out of my driveway and headed toward Castle Rock, Jeff, Trice, and I did the only logical thing we could think of. We jumped into my Camaro and followed them in secret.

Before the three of us hit the road, I grabbed a baseball bat from the bedroom closet and the tire iron from the trunk. If things got violent, we wanted to be armed. Our plan was to arrive at the designated meeting place in Castle Rock shortly after Chuck and L.B. did. The timing of this would be tricky, but we needed to give Chuck and L.B. enough of a headstart so they wouldn't see us following them. My Camaro had a custom red paint job, and its appearance was unmistakable. If Chuck caught a glimpse of my car in his rearview mirror, the jig would be up. None of us had ever been to Castle Rock, but Jeff knew his way around Colorado better than any of us and had gone over the directions with Chuck and L.B. before they had left. He was confident that he could get us there without any problem.

Chuck and L.B. arrived at the meeting place about fifteen minutes before we did. Just as planned, the meeting with the middleman took place in the parking lot of an abandoned factory on the outskirts of Castle Rock. After Chuck and L.B. arrived at their destination and parked the car in the lot, a rusty Buick LeSabre pulled up behind them. Driving the Buick was the middleman. The original plan was for Chuck and the middleman to meet alone, but neither side had kept their end of the bargain. Both of them had brought along an escort. Another man was sitting in the Buick's front passenger seat, and L.B. was sitting with Chuck in the Mazda.

After Chuck spoke to the middleman (who was tall and thin and wearing sunglasses and a stocking cap) and showed him the roll of bills, the man reciprocated by showing him the bin of stolen microphones. The bin was stashed inside the Buick's trunk. While Chuck was looking over the microphones, he glanced through the Buick's rear window and noticed two guitar cases lying across the back seat. The middleman had brought all the stolen equipment with him.

Upon seeing the cases, Chuck couldn't help himself. Without thinking things through, he rushed to the side of the car, opened the rear door, and attempted to remove the cases from the vehicle. When the middleman saw what Chuck was doing, he bolted over, grabbed him by the arm, and pulled him away from the car. Chuck pushed the man away, and the two of them started shouting at each other.

Just as this was happening, Trice, Jeff, and I arrived on the scene. The road leading down to the parking lot was at the top of a hill, and as we approached, we had a good view of what was going on. We could clearly see that Chuck and the middleman were in the middle of a heated argument. I pressed down on the Camaro's gas pedal as hard as I dared, and we went racing down the hill toward them.

As we reached the bottom of the hill and swung into the parking lot, I slammed on the brakes and came to a screeching halt. Jeff grabbed the baseball bat, and I killed the engine and grabbed the tire iron. The three of us jumped out of the Camaro and rushed up to the scene. As we did this, the man sitting inside the Buick got out of the vehicle. He pulled a handgun and pointed it at Chuck's head. But this only enraged Chuck further, and he started walking toward the man who was holding the gun. Upon seeing what was happening, L.B. jumped out of the Mazda and pleaded for the man to put the gun away. But the middleman pulled a gun of his own and started waving it around wildly. Then he pointed the gun in my direction and demanded that we drop our weapons. We were hesitant to do so, but a baseball bat and a tire iron were no match for handguns.

With no other choice, we dropped our weapons to the ground. Upon seeing that we were in the line of fire, Chuck finally backed off. The middleman motioned to his accomplice to join him next to the Buick, and the two men started whispering to each other. They appeared very anxious. The men raised their handguns again, but this time they pointed them in the direction of my Camaro. Upon seeing this, I started wondering if someone else had arrived on the scene, maybe the police, so I turned around and looked behind me. No one was there. There was nothing behind us except for the Camaro, which was empty.

I turned around and saw that the men were still pointing their guns at my car. I also saw that they no longer looked anxious. Now they appeared to be frightened of something. Still pointing their guns, the men hurriedly climbed back inside the Buick. The old car's engine roared to life, and the two men sped away in a cloud of dust and smoke.

The five of us stood in the parking lot long after the men were gone trying to figure out what had just happened. We were confused as to why the men had acted so strangely, and our confusion plagued us during the entire trip back home. After arriving back at my house in Fort Collins, we all admitted that the confrontation in Castle Rock had left us mentally and physically exhausted and that we needed to get some rest. On his way out the door, I told Chuck I was sorry that we hadn't been able to get his equipment back but that the most important thing was that none of us had been shot or killed. He agreed and pointed out that guitars and microphones were easy to replace, but that best friends and bandmates were not.

A week later, Chuck showed up at my house for band rehearsal with a guitar case hanging from each of his hands.

In one of the cases was his Gibson Les Paul and in the other case was his Ibanez Iceman. In the Mazda's trunk was the bin of stolen microphones. When I asked Chuck how he had managed to get his equipment back, he told me that a few days earlier he had received another phone call from the middleman. Chuck said that during their conversation the man had admitted to being the thief and that he had decided it was in his best interest to return the stolen equipment. He told Chuck that he had come to this decision because he didn't want any trouble with the man in the gray suit that had been sitting behind the wheel of my Camaro during the failed negotiations in Castle Rock.

The Entropy Sequence

Shortly after the gig in Colorado Springs, Chuck started dating a former high school sweetheart of his named Angelica Vogel. Angelica (whom everyone called Angie) was a beautiful and strong-willed young woman of German descent. As I clearly recall, Angie was very proud of her heritage and used it to her advantage by drinking the members of Entropy under the table on a regular basis.

Although Chuck was open to having Angie attend rehearsals and hang around with the members of the band, he was guarded about her exposure to The Force. He was adamant that any in-depth discussions on the topic of our otherworldly friend not take place in Angie's presence, or in the presence of anyone else for that matter. Chuck knew that keeping Angie totally out of the loop was impossible, but on the other hand he didn't want her to be privy to an overabundance of information on the subject. Discussions in front of Angie about numbers, poems, and dreams were just fine, but the topics of The Force and the gray man were strictly taboo.

Chuck was becoming obsessed with shielding our knowledge of The Force from the outside world. And it was because of this obsession that I started noticing the subtle changes that were taking place in all of our behavior. The five of us were in the early stages of becoming very different people than we had been just a few months earlier. Not only was Chuck becoming more and more obsessive, he was becoming aggressive. His martial arts training combined with our alignment with The Force had made him cocky and unpredictable. It had made him fearless, and his fearlessness was evident in how he was interacting with people he considered outsiders. If Chuck met someone at a party or on the street that he didn't like, he wasn't afraid to say so to the person's face. Chuck had also stepped up his drinking, which was making matters even worse.

L.B. was changing as well, and not entirely for the better. His musicianship and drumming skills had improved considerably over the last year, and these abilities had made him practically narcissistic. He started acting disrespectful toward his parents and other members of his family for seemingly no other reason than the fact that he could get away with it. He was changing girlfriends almost as often as he was changing his socks, and I was catching him telling white lies to his friends and bandmates.

But I should also point out that in most ways Chuck and L.B. were still fantastic and talented young men. I just couldn't help but wonder how many of the changes I was seeing in them were a result of our association with the gray man. And speaking of our otherworldly friend, I was noticing changes taking place in his behavior as well. Until recently, the power of The Force had been contained inside my home and inside of us. But we had unwittingly given the gray man license to roam, and he was using this newfound freedom to do whatever he pleased. He had followed us to the gig in Colorado Springs. He had used his power to manipulate our audience and to prevent Shelby and Janice from being injured in a car accident. He had revealed himself to the thief and scared him badly enough to return Chuck's equipment. None of the things the gray man had done were necessarily bad, but because of them I started wondering if we had created a monster. I couldn't help but wonder how large the monster would eventually become and to what extent it would use its power.

But all of my wondering aside, I knew that the five members of Entropy were an integral part of that power, and that if it became too large to contain, we would have no one to blame but ourselves. All I could do now was hope that it would never come down to that. But in truth, it wasn't the changes I had noticed in Chuck, L.B., or even the gray man that worried me the most. It was the changes taking place within Trice and myself that had me deeply concerned.

September 1981

By late summer of 1981, Trice was practically living at my house, and we had become diligent students of entropy and The Force. Trice and I were closer than ever, and our friendship had blossomed into a deep bond with one another. During our studies, we learned some fascinating things about the science of entropy and the myriad theories on the subject. We learned that entropy (also known as the second law of thermodynamics) is the measurement of the amount of disorder in a system. We also learned that entropy influences a system's available energy and the ability of the energy to do work. Another theory about entropy (and of great interest to me in particular) is the hypothesis that entropy represents the amount of information contained in a message. But the theory about entropy that captivated us the most is known as the arrow of time.

British astronomer Arthur Eddington coined the term "arrow of time" in 1927 as a way to describe the asymmetry, or "single direction," of time. As it relates to thermodynamics, the arrow of time demonstrates that the amount of entropy in a system tends to increase over time, and as entropy increases, so does the amount of disorder. From this perspective, the measurement of the amount of entropy in a system is a way to distinguish the past from the future. If the direction of time is constant and singular, all phenomena can be linked back to the second law of thermodynamics.

During our studies, I eventually came to the conclusion that if the arrow of time theory was correct, the amount of entropy and disorder in the universe would increase exponentially until the universe and everything within it was destroyed. Or, as Trice and I used to put it, "One day entropy will claim itself." And it was because of the arrow of time theory that Trice and I learned how to make direct contact with the gray man.

One day as Trice and I were sitting at my kitchen table having our usual conversations about entropy and The Force, something happened that forever changed the way in which we were able to communicate with the gray man, something that was as simple as it was profound. As Trice and I were sitting there talking, I brought up my theory about how one day entropy would claim itself and destroy the universe.

As I was speaking, an interesting thought floated into my mind. I looked across the table at Trice and said, "Entropy can be reversed if a person believes in certain things." I was holding my notebook in my hand, and I casually tossed it onto the table and looked out the kitchen window. My eyes came to rest on the crown of a tree far in the distance. I couldn't keep my eyes or my mind off of that tree. I started hearing a faint buzzing sound and felt the sensation of lost space and time. Suddenly my consciousness was no longer in my own body but in the crown of that distant tree. I felt exactly the same as I had the day that I was given the poem and Trice and I made the long walk back home.

What I was seeing and feeling was beyond beautiful. I felt like my entire being had been broken down into millions of pieces and that my life energy and the energy of the tree were as one. I could no longer distinguish myself from anything else. But at the same time, I also sensed that I was only a small part of a larger whole.

I remained in this altered state for about forty-five seconds, and then my consciousness was pulled back inside my body. I turned my gaze from the window and looked at Trice, who was still sitting across the table from me. My notebook was lying open on the table in front of him, and he was holding a pencil in his hand. Trice was staring at me as though I had lost my mind. Or, to be more precise, he was staring at me as though I were an alien from another world. I was confused as to why Trice was staring at me so strangely. I shrugged my shoulders and asked, "What?"

Still staring, Trice raised an eyebrow and said, "Can you say that again?"

"Say what?" I asked. "Oh," I continued, "you mean about entropy being reversed?"

"No," Trice answered. "Everything you said after that."

Now I was really confused. After my statement about entropy being reversed, I hadn't spoken another word. Or so I thought. From my perspective, I had only been in the trancelike state for about forty-five seconds. But for Trice, over fifteen minutes had passed. According to Trice, after making the statement about entropy, I had tossed the notebook down on the table and stared out the window, just like I remembered.

But a few minutes later, according to Trice, I turned to face him and started speaking again. Trice said that at first the things I was saying seemed to make perfect sense, but then he realized that what I was saying didn't make any sense at all. Trice told me that I had spoken aloud a series of unrelated words, and that between the words I had rattled off a sequence of numbers and mathematical equations. He told me that the words and numbers were coming out of my mouth so fast that they were almost impossible to comprehend. I couldn't remember doing or saying any of these things. But what disturbed me the most was that Trice also told me that while I was speaking, the color of my eyes had grown darker and darker until they were nearly black. My eyes had also turned black the day that Chuck and I had followed the map up the stairs and discovered the portal.

With Trice's assistance, over the next two months I learned how to enter into this trancelike state at will. I also learned that being in the trance allowed the gray man to speak to Trice through me. By working together, Trice and I discovered that the random words and numbers I would speak meant absolutely nothing, but that the mathematical equations were an advanced form of the numerical language the gray man had used to speak to us from the very beginning.

For the purposes of translation and documentation, we made it a habit to record the trance sessions on my reel-to-reel tape recorder. While listening to the playback, we discovered that the solutions to the mathematical equations were never higher than the number 26 and that each solution corresponded to a letter in the alphabet. For example, if during one on my trances Trice would ask the gray man a question and the answer was yes, the solutions to the equations we were given would be the numbers 25 (Y), 5 (E), and 19 (S). If the answer was no, the solutions would be the numbers 14 (N) and 15 (O).

The answers to more complex questions were often given to us in anagrams and involved conceptual mathematical equations, so for obvious reasons they were much more difficult to solve. I'd hated math ever since my school days and was never any good at it, so it fell on Trice's shoulders to solve the more complex equations. I was much better at unscrambling the anagrams than doing the math, anyway.

Even though we were able to successfully decipher all of the messages we were given, only roughly half of them made any sense. I chalked this up to something being lost in translation. However, not all of the information that was relayed to us was in the form of answers. During many of the trance sessions we were also given two distinct commands. Although the exact wording of the commands was never identical, they had a repeating theme. The first command was that the members of Entropy were to go west to California and the heart of the music industry. The second command was that under no circumstances were we to show others our darker side. And it was this second command that caused extreme anxiety for Trice.

Due to the implications of the second command, Trice became a very conflicted person. As I mentioned before, Trice had been raised in a Christian household, and even though his religious views had changed over the years, he was now struggling to find a very delicate balance between his inner rock 'n' roll bad boy and his fundamental spiritual beliefs. His desires and religious principles were at odds with each other and were engaged in an internal tug of war.

Trice had come to the conclusion that the words "darker side" in the command implied something evil. He started leaning toward the belief that the gray man was a demon or perhaps even Satan himself. This demonic force, Trice alleged, was the darker side that we had been commanded not to reveal to outsiders. But I disagreed with Trice, and it was because of our opposing points of view that a rift began to form between us.

I personally believed that the darker side that was referred to in the command wasn't a demonic presence, but rather the darker side of human nature—the darker sides of the five members of Entropy to be exact. The gray man was powerful, without question, but I had never sensed anything inherently evil in him, at least no more so than I had in anything else.

Even though at the time I was still a fledgling student of the supernatural, I was aware enough of my situation and my surroundings to come to my own conclusion on the matter. I concluded that good and evil were an inseparable part of each other and that the true balance between them was held within humanity, not between a god and a devil. Trice and I debated this subject without end, and as hard as we tried, we could find no middle ground on the subject.

Trice tried to persuade me that his was the stronger opinion due to the fact that he had a much more extensive background in religion than I did. I countered Trice's argument by pointing out that the gray man had never materialized in front of him and that Trice didn't fully understand what it felt like to be in his presence. The debate raged on and on, but Trice and I eventually realized that we were acting like prepubescent teenagers engaged in a cockfight and that neither of us had hard evidence to back up our case. Theological differences aside, we were still friends and bandmates, and in the end we shook hands, agreed to disagree, and vowed to not let it affect our music or our camaraderie. Just as balance must be maintained between good and evil, we knew that it was up to us to find an equilibrium between ourselves.

But even though Trice and I had promised each other that we would put forth our best efforts to not allow our differences in opinion to affect our friendship, deep down inside I knew that it was already too late. The damage was done, and the cracks in the foundation of Entropy were beginning to show.

Of the five of us, Jeff alone seemed to be immune to the changes that were taking place in our beliefs and our behaviors. In many ways, Jeff had a more intimate understanding of the supernatural than any of us did, and this intimacy somehow shielded him from the brunt of the mental effects that being a part of The Force were creating in the other members of Entropy. What we didn't know at the time was that Jeff wouldn't exhibit the symptoms or adverse affects in his behavior until many years later.

Our alignment with the gray man had brought about mental changes in L.B. and Chuck and spiritual changes in Trice. But the changes that were taking place inside of me were of the paranormal variety. At first, the changes I was experiencing were subtle, so for the most part I brushed them off as coincidence or simply ignored them altogether. But despite my initial indifference, the truth was that I had developed a strange, new talent. I found myself answering the front door before visitors had a chance to knock. I would reach for the phone three seconds before it rang. I caught my subconscious playing out the words to television ads or the tune to a radio jingle minutes before they were broadcast over the airwaves.

In the beginning, these things were easy for me to write off as quirks of nature, but eventually the episodes became so intense that I could no longer ignore them. Before long

I was answering the phone before it even rang, and I knew whose voice I would hear on the other end of the line. I jumped from being able to predict when ads and jingles would be played over the television and radio to knowing in advance the exact dialogue of live broadcasts and unscheduled, late-breaking news reports.

But things really didn't hit home for me until the night a childhood friend of mine named Nick Riley died. I hadn't seen Nick for over eleven years, nor had I really thought that much about him during that time. Yet one night while I was sitting in my living room watching TV, an indescribable feeling washed over me, and in that moment I knew that Nick had been killed. I had been given a revelation of the end of his life. The vision I had seen was unclear, but nonetheless I was certain that Nick had been killed in a traffic accident.

After seeing this horrible vision, I immediately jumped up from the couch and ran over to the desk in search of a phone book. I remembered that Nick's mother's name was Emma, and I was able to locate a single listing for an Emma Riley in the book. I dialed the number, and Nick's mother answered on the first ring. She was able to answer so quickly because she had just hung up the phone after speaking with a policeman who had informed her that her son had been killed in a motorcycle accident on the outskirts of Denver.

After speaking with Nick's mother and hanging up the phone, I sat at the desk for well over an hour trying to figure out what was happening to me. Even though at the time I didn't have an understanding of psychic abilities, I came to the conclusion that what I was experiencing had to be a form of clairvoyance. Up until a month earlier, I had never experienced anything even resembling a psychic episode, but I now possessed a very real extrasensory ability. The only question was, how?

Thinking this question through, I narrowed the possibilities down to a single theory. I theorized that on the day Chuck and I had discovered the map and I had seen into the portal at the top of the stairs, a part of the gray man had transferred into me and remained. I theorized that, intentionally or not, during that encounter a sliver of the gray man's powers was passed on to me. As absurd as it sounded even to me, it was the only theory that made sense. I concluded that if clairvoyance was merely a symptom of being a part of The Force, then my bandmates would be developing this same ability. And so far, not a single one of them had.

The bottom line was that a part of my brain had been rewired into a sort of extrasensory antenna and that the rewiring had heightened my connection to The Force to such an extreme that I was losing my sense of self. A small part of me was starting to feel like I was being used as a tool, like I was little more than a sideshow in the gray man's circus. But even if this were true, I was still an integral part of the performance. And without question, the gray man's circus was the greatest show on earth.

CHRONICLE FOUR
The Darker Side

Show others not your darker side,
for then you must stay here.
—THE GRAY MAN

A Ghost of a Chance

By January of 1982, Entropy was playing shows on a regular basis, but none of the gigs were anywhere near as large or grand as the one in Colorado Springs had been. Jack Forman had prebooked Entropy to play at the next year's festival, but that show wouldn't take place for over four months and the five of us were getting anxious about the band's prospects for the immediate future.

The command for Entropy to go to California that had been given to us by the gray man was always open for discussion, but we hadn't been able to come up with a realistic plan on how to accomplish that feat. We typically discussed this matter in the early morning hours during breakfasts the five of us would have at local diners after playing shows. By the time we were done playing and had our equipment loaded, it was always very early in the morning, and going to breakfast gave us a chance to unwind and get some much needed food in our stomachs. It also gave us the chance to sober up before driving home. One morning while we were having such a breakfast, opportunity not only came knocking on our door, it kicked it wide open.

One night while Entropy was headlining a show at a nightclub in Boulder, unbeknownst to us there was a very special person in the audience. This person was a promoter from Denver named Chris Thompson, and he had come to the show just to hear us play. Chris was a good-looking man in his late twenties and had plenty of cash to throw around. He had intended to speak with us immediately after we left the stage but got distracted by two attractive young ladies in the audience, and by then we had already packed up our gear and hit the road.

After Chris made a few inquiries, one of the bartenders that knew us well and was familiar with our habits directed him to a local diner where he would most likely be able to track us down. While we were talking and drinking coffee, Chris walked into the diner and introduced himself to us. We invited Chris to join us at the table, and he sat down and started talking.

We quickly discovered that Chris wasn't just a promoter from Denver, he was *the* promoter from Denver. Chris informed us that he had cut his teeth in the music industry working for an entertainment agency in Chicago, and after moving to Colorado, he had promoted quite a few bands that went on to become well-known recording artists. He told us that a current project he was working on involved showcasing Colorado musicians for top-shelf entertainment agencies, international promoters, and even the heads of record companies.

Chris went on to tell us that he had been given a copy of our demo tape from a fellow promoter and had heard about the show in Colorado Springs. Chris had been impressed enough by our demo tape to hunt us down, and he was interested in booking Entropy for some shows in Denver. He told us that if the Denver shows went smoothly and the band was well received, he would be more than happy to feature Entropy in one of his showcases.

Chris thought we might even have a shot at the most coveted prize a band from the Rocky Mountains could ever hope for: the chance to open for a major musical act at Red Rocks Amphitheatre in Morrison, Colorado. The members of Entropy had attended many concerts at Red Rocks in the past and knew that the amphitheatre was hands down the most beautiful setting for a show anywhere in the state, and quite possibly in the entire country. Having a shot at opening for a major act at Red Rocks was the opportunity of a lifetime. Upon hearing this fantastic news, it took everything we had to contain ourselves and not jump up on the table and break into song. We told Chris that of course we would be interested in considering any and all possibilities and that we were delighted that he had taken such an interest in the band.

Chris suggested that the first step would be to have Entropy come to Denver and attend one of his showcases so we could get a feel for what was involved and groom ourselves for our own showcase. He also offered to show us around some of the venues that he was currently booking other acts into. Chris informed us that he had a couple area bands scheduled for a showcase in two weeks and recommended that we attend that performance. He told us that if we decided to go to the show, he would be more than happy to put us up for the weekend at his house so we didn't have to make a round-trip drive back home or pay for hotel rooms.

We made arrangements to make the trip to Denver on the spot and told Chris that we would see him in two weeks' time. The promoter bid us a good night and left the diner. As the door closed behind him, our enthusiasm got the better of us and we got so loud and boisterous that we were almost thrown out of the diner.

Pandora's Box

The collective energy of Entropy was at an all-time high, and the air was thick with anticipation. The two weeks leading up to our trip to Denver should have crawled by, but they passed by quickly, and before we knew it we were on the road and headed for the city. The five of us were as nervous as we were excited. We would soon be taking our first few steps on the road that other bands had blazed before us. This road could potentially lead us to everything we'd ever desired. We knew that if this road was traveled tirelessly and with purpose, it might eventually lead to fame.

Chris's home was located in a suburb of Denver called Arvada, and as we arrived at our destination, we got a small taste of what the acquisition of fame could mean. More often than not, fame and fortune go hand in hand, and even though Chris admitted that he hadn't acquired much fame outside of Colorado, he had certainly acquired his share of wealth. Chris's home was absolutely gorgeous, and directly behind it was an unobscured view of the mountains. A sandstone driveway led to a garage on either side of the house and was surrounded by enormous boulders and lush (albeit snow-covered) landscaping. The house itself was a modern two-story situated on an acre of land and featured a walk-out basement carved into the side of a hill. The sight of Chris's home from the outside was something to behold, but the inside was even better.

After meeting us at the front door and inviting us inside, Chris offered us some drinks from his bar and gave us the grand tour. The house's ceilings were impossibly high, and marble flooring extended throughout most of the house. Chris led the five of us through an enormous dining hall and a gourmet kitchen. The number of rooms seemed endless, and I remember losing count along the way. Chris was unmarried and had no children, and I was having a hard time imagining what one person would do with so much space. But the one thing I wasn't having a hard time imagining was having such a home for myself. Chris was a self-made man, and if he could do it, so could we. It was simply a matter of talent, determination, and a hell of a lot of work.

After the tour, the six of us went to Chris's back porch (which ate up more square footage than my entire house) and had a few more drinks while sitting around his outdoor fire pit. Chris told us that if it was okay with us, he planned to take the band out to dinner at one of his favorite restaurants in Denver before going to the showcase. We thanked Chris for the generous offer and told him we would be delighted to join him for dinner. Two hours later as we were preparing to leave for Denver, I noticed that L.B. was nowhere to be found.

After searching a good portion of the house for L.B., I finally found him outside. He was standing at the end of the driveway and talking to one of Chris's neighbor's sons, who appeared to be around our same age. I called out to L.B. and told him that it was time to go. L.B. gave me a nod and called back that he would be there shortly. A few minutes later, L.B. joined us in Chris's living room and told us that he wasn't feeling well. He said that as much as he wanted to go to dinner and the show, he simply wasn't feeling up to it.

Chris told L.B. that he understood and that it wasn't a problem. He showed L.B. a bedroom where he could get some rest and told him to make himself at home. Chris added that if he got hungry, he was welcome to anything he could find in the kitchen. As the rest of us headed out the door, L.B. sat down on the couch in Chris's living room to watch some TV.

It was a crisp but beautiful night in Denver, and after having an incredible dinner in lower downtown (known locally as LoDo), we spent some time walking around the city and taking in the sights. I had never been in downtown Denver during the evening hours before, and the city was alive with the sights and sounds of nightlife. The urban landscape hummed with the sounds of voices and traffic and was lit by flashing lights and the vibrant glow of neon signs.

We eventually returned to Chris's car and made the short drive to a place called the Mammoth Gardens Theatre. Mammoth Gardens, previously known as the Fillmore Auditorium, opened its doors in 1907 and over the years served as everything from a roller rink to a concert hall. At one time the building had even housed the Fritchle Automobile & Battery Company. Chris informed us that the

Fillmore's name had been changed to Mammoth Gardens a little over a year earlier in 1981 and that it was once again a home to music.

The Mammoth was where Chris's showcase was taking place. After Chris had set us up with VIP passes, he led us inside the theatre. Much to our surprise, the Mammoth still retained much of the Fillmore's old-world charm. The theatre was spacious, and much of the building's original architecture remained intact. Beautiful crystal chandeliers hung from the ceiling, enhancing the quaint atmosphere. The stage filled the entire back wall and was almost as large as the one we had played on in Colorado Springs.

Before we arrived at the theatre, Chris had told us that he was showcasing two bands that evening and that both of them were from the Denver metro area. The first act being showcased was a progressive band called Pages, and the second act was a power-rock trio called Crusader. Chris told us that he had some details to see to backstage before the show started and that he would catch up with us a while later. Before Chris headed backstage, he handed us some drink tickets and told us to mingle as we pleased. He also warned us not to be too surprised if we ran into someone famous in the audience.

The showcase started at a little past nine in the evening, and Pages was the first act to perform. The band consisted of five musicians who appeared to be in their late thirties. Pages' music was unquestionably tight and they had some solid originals, but the band was a bit pretentious for my taste and I wasn't sad to see their performance come to an end.

Around thirty minutes after Pages' set ended, Crusader took the stage. Crusader was made up of an eclectic group of musicians and was much more to my liking. They were younger than Pages, and their music was considerably heavier. All in all, the four of us enjoyed the show, but in my opinion neither of the bands came close to topping Entropy. Their originals were decent but lacked spark. Neither Crusader nor Pages possessed our songwriting talent or charisma. That much was obvious in how they were received by the audience. Not unlike us, the audience had been amused by the performances but not thoroughly entertained. The showcase itself was professional and well sponsored, but if bands like Pages and Crusader were the best the Denver music scene had to offer, I was confident that it wouldn't be long before Entropy was kicking ass and taking names.

Shortly after the show ended, Chris rejoined us and we spent the next hour following him around the auditorium and meeting people. No record company execs had attended the showcase, but there were plenty of other promoters and theatre owners in the crowd. All in all, we'd had a great time at Chris's showcase and had done a considerable amount of networking, which we knew might pay off big time in the near future.

After having one last drink at the bar, Chris suggested that we head back to his place so we could get settled in for the night. We were all tired and reasonably buzzed by that point, and we agreed that getting some rest might be a good idea. Around thirty minutes later, we were back in Arvada and pulling into Chris's driveway. As we got out of the car and were walking up to the front door, we saw that there was a party going on at Chris's house. This wouldn't have been all that unusual expect for the fact that it wasn't Chris's party. It was L.B.'s.

As the five of us walked through the front door, we saw that there were people everywhere inside Chris's house. And I do mean everywhere. There were at least fifteen young adults standing in the kitchen and a handful more sitting at the dining room table snacking on potato chips and drinking beer. Even more people were helping themselves to liquor at Chris's bar. We could hear voices coming from the rooms upstairs, and we found out a while later that a young couple was having sex in Chris's bedroom.

As we stood in the foyer trying to wrap our minds around what was happening, three young men who appeared to be around my age came rushing up to us and extended their hands. They looked us over from head to toe and told us that they had seen us many times in concert and were huge fans of the band. I would have been deeply honored if it weren't for the fact that Entropy wasn't the band they were talking about.

After a short conversation with the men, I discovered that they had mistaken Entropy for a major musical act of the time. That musical act was none other than British rockers Def Leppard. L.B. and myself in particular bore a striking resemblance to Def Leppard's drummer and rhythm guitarist, so mistaking us for them was entirely understandable. What made the case of mistaken identity even more understandable was the fact that it wasn't uncommon for Chris to entertain famous musicians at his home. But what I didn't understand was what happened next.

After denying that I was the guitarist for Def Leppard, the men became agitated and called me everything short of a liar. The conversation got more and more heated, but during our talk I got the lowdown on how the case of mistaken identity had come to pass. Apparently, earlier in the day one of Chris's neighbor's sons had mistaken L.B. for Def Leppard's drummer. That was the same neighbor I had seen L.B. speaking with before the rest of us had left for the showcase in Denver. Although L.B. had never admitted to being Def Leppard's drummer, he hadn't denied it either.

For a reason I have never fully understood, L.B. took full advantage of the case of mistaken identity. He had played along with it for one of the stupidest and most self-centered reasons imaginable. He had done it to look like a big shot and to feed his own ego. Still denying that I was a famous rock star, I thanked the young men for the information and went in search of L.B.

I found L.B. sitting on the couch in Chris's living room, surrounded by his adoring fans. Or, to put it more accurately, he was surrounded by Def Leppard's adoring fans. As I stepped into the room, I overheard him talking about our (Def Leppard's) stage show and the number of semi-trucks it took to haul our equipment from show to show. And if that wasn't bad enough, he was also talking about something much, much worse. He was talking about the gray man and The Force.

Before I could get a single word out of my mouth, Chuck and Chris came storming into the living room. Upon seeing our drummer and hearing what he was talking about, Chuck walked up to the couch and grabbed L.B. by the collar of his shirt. He hoisted him up and off the couch and said, "Shut your fucking mouth!"

The entire situation was a nightmare. Chris was somewhere between anger and rage. His face was bright red, and the man literally looked like he might explode at any second. He was beyond furious about the unauthorized party and L.B.'s deception. He started screaming for everyone to get the hell out of his house. And not surprisingly, "everyone" included the members of Entropy.

After all of the partygoers had gone, we tried our best to apologize to Chris for the misunderstanding, but our words weren't well received. Chris told us that as long as L.B. was in the band, we could forget about him booking us any gigs in Denver or playing in his showcases. As far as Chris Thompson was concerned, Entropy was blacklisted. Still apologizing to no gain, the five of us gathered our belongings, walked out of Chris's front door for the last time, and headed for home.

Trice, Jeff, and I made the drive back to Fort Collins in my Camaro, and L.B. rode with Chuck in the Mazda. Chuck had a few choice words for our drummer and had insisted that L.B. ride back with him. That was just fine with the rest of us. We were well beyond pissed, and for the time being, we didn't care to be in L.B.'s presence.

Sometime later, Chuck told us that during the drive home, L.B. had broken down into tears and had expressed great shame for his actions. He had also pleaded with Chuck to try to convince the rest of us not to throw him out of the band. L.B. knew how angry we were and realized that the four of us handing him his walking papers was a very real possibility.

On the ride home, L.B. had also admitted to Chuck that even he himself didn't understand why he had done what he had done. The closest he could come to explaining his actions was that he had wanted to know what it was like to be famous. But by doing so, he had pretty much blown any chance he'd had at acquiring fame himself. As much as the rest of us could relate to his desire for fame, it was a lousy excuse, and the inevitable debates about whether or not to remove L.B. from the band began to take place outside of his presence. There were even discussions about whether the band should stay together at all. If word got out about the incident, it would destroy our reputation in Denver before we even had a chance to earn it. The incident had damaged our credibility and placed roadblocks on the path to our own fame that would be very difficult to overcome.

The debates about what to do raged on and on without consensus, but I was the bandleader and in the end the guys looked to me to make the final decision on L.B.'s fate. L.B. had fucked up bad, but the one thing I knew about making it in rock 'n' roll was that by far the majority of the bands that had made it big all had one thing in common: perfect musical chemistry. Most well-known rock acts hated each other and didn't get along offstage, but onstage and in the studio it was a completely different story. Despite their differences and personality clashes, these bands excelled onstage and in the studio. The chances of Entropy finding another drummer who could replicate L.B.'s style and chemistry were slim to none. Throwing L.B. out of the band carried with it the very real possibility that we would never find another drummer who was capable of replacing him.

Even though L.B.'s mistake bordered on being unforgivable, he was still my bandmate and my friend. I had one hell of a decision to make, and either choice had consequences. I told the guys that I needed a hiatus from the band to get my head straight and reach a decision. It was mutually agreed that Entropy would take a minimum of one month's time away from performing and rehearsing. The break would give us some much-needed time away from each other as well as time to reflect upon what

Entropy really meant to us. If the band had any hope of staying together, some personal space and soul searching were crucial.

The Downward Spiral
March 1982

Trice and I hadn't spoken to our other bandmates in weeks, but during the hiatus we spent most of our free time together. We used this time to search for answers and to figure out our next move. We were both very happy that Entropy hadn't imploded and still had a chance of staying together, but regardless of L.B.'s apology and pledge to never again do anything to dishonor himself or the band, we were having doubts about Entropy's chances to endure.

Despite our ever-widening differences in opinion about the gray man and The Force, Trice and I conspired to go to California on our own if the situation got any worse or if Entropy disbanded. Over the previous few weeks, we had attempted to contact and confer with the gray man many times without success. Even though I was able to attain the trance state, our otherworldly counterpart was silent. The gray man was no longer speaking through me, nor were we seeing sequential numbers on the clock or any other signs of his presence. It was obvious that the gray man was either as upset about the band's situation as we were or refused to get involved.

Trice and I were on our own without The Force to guide us. We sequestered ourselves inside my home and pored over the lyrics we had written over the previous two years in search of clues or hidden meanings we might have missed, but we found nothing. We were so self-absorbed and desperate for answers that we hadn't seen or spoken to Shelby and Janice in weeks. As the days went by, our girlfriends were becoming less and less important to us. All that mattered was finding a way to make things right again. All that mattered was finding a way back to Entropy and The Force.

After more than a month of internal debate, I made the decision to allow L.B. to stay in the band. But I also made him swear on everything he held sacred that he would never do anything like the stunt he had pulled at Chris's home in Arvada ever again. L.B. agreed to my terms, and the five of us came to the consensus that it was time to let bygones be bygones and for the band to start playing together once again. We had a lot of lost ground to make up for both musically and spiritually, and it was time to get the band back in gear.

We scheduled a rehearsal for the next Saturday at nine o'clock in the evening, which was two days away. If at all possible, we preferred to rehearse at nighttime rather than during the day. Not unlike most rock 'n' roll bands, Entropy thrived at night. Trice and I spent the two days leading up to the rehearsal jamming together in the basement, limbering up our fingers and getting back in the groove. The weekend finally arrived, and the guys showed up at my house at nine o'clock on the dot, just as we had planned.

Upon answering the door and inviting my bandmates inside, I saw that they weren't alone. Chuck had brought along his girlfriend, Angie, and L.B. had brought along a young friend of his named Jon whom we had never met before. I was instantly torn about Jon and Angie being present for our rehearsal. On the one hand, I saw it as an intrusion on a very important night in the band's survival. But on the other hand, I knew that having guests might just inspire us to throw off the weight of past events and get down to business. I decided to hold my tongue and allow Jon and Angie to stay.

It was exciting to have the band back together again, and before we got around to rehearsing we spent a good deal of time chatting and downing a few drinks. By the time we got down to the basement and had our equipment warmed up, it was a little past eleven o'clock at night. As was usually the case whenever she attended our rehearsals, Angie stayed upstairs in my living room sitting in an easy chair with the television cranked as loud as it would go. Down in the basement, I invited Jon to have a seat on one of the couches next to Jeff. Chuck, Trice, and I strapped on our guitars, and L.B. took his place behind his drum set.

After a short debate about which song we should play first, we decided on Jeff's personal favorite, "Tamin' the Wood." L.B. clacked his drumsticks together four times, and we started playing for the first time in what had felt like ages. But two bars into the song, I could tell that something was off. Playing together should have felt fantastic and stimulating, but it didn't feel that way at all. It felt dull, like the edge of an overused knife.

A major component of Entropy was missing, and I knew exactly what that component was. The gray man was absent and had been for many weeks now. And because he was absent, so was The Force. I should have felt like a seasoned musician, but instead I felt like I had many years earlier. I felt just like I had the day I took my first music lesson from Chuck, sitting in his basement with a guitar pick taped to my injured thumb and struggling to play my first few chords.

The music we were playing felt old and lifeless. The magic that we had worked so hard to create was gone. Looking into my bandmates' eyes, I could tell they were feeling the same things that I was feeling. They looked forlorn and lost, like they were attending a funeral rather than rocking out in my basement.

Despite all of this, we continued playing, perhaps hoping that the next song would be better than the last. But as we neared the end of our set list, I could tell that it simply wasn't going to happen. It was getting late, and I knew that it would take a miracle to breathe life back into the room. A miracle—or a force from another world.

At around twelve fifteen in the morning, there was a single song remaining on our set list. That song was "Old

Number Seveign." The song was almost entirely instrumental and ended with one of L.B.'s typically brilliant drum solos. Near the end of the song, the rest of us would be able sit down on the couches and listen to our drummer play. "Old Number Seveign" started out feeling and sounding much better than the other songs in the set, and as L.B.'s drum solo neared, I could feel the energy in the room growing stronger. I started thinking that we might yet be able to recapture what we had lost and that maybe there was hope for Entropy after all.

The time came for L.B. to work his magic behind the drum kit, and we unstrapped our guitars and joined Jon and Jeff on the couches. Trice took a seat at the end of the couch that was nearest to the doorway leading in and out of the basement. Sitting next to him were Jon and Jeff. Chuck and I sat down on the couch that was in the corner of the room. L.B. started playing his solo, and I was delighted to hear that his drumming was as brilliant as ever. Listening to him play made me forget all about his past misdeeds.

I'd heard L.B.'s drum solo so many times in the past that I knew it beat for beat, and he was playing it just as I remembered it. Everyone in the room was enjoying it immensely. But for some unknown reason, in the middle of the solo, L.B. just stopped playing. An odd look washed over his face, and his brow furrowed. He crossed his arms, lowered his head, and stared down at his feet. He just sat there on his drum throne without speaking a word. Three minutes later, L.B. raised his head and scanned the room with his eyes. The look in his eyes was distant and other-worldly. He looked just like he had the morning after he'd had the strange dream in the guest room and Trice and I had been awakened by the sound of his laughter.

L.B. took in a tremendous breath and leaned back on his throne. He slowly turned his head from right to left, looking each and every one of us directly in the eye with a piercing gaze. He exhaled with a breathy hiss and said, "Let me mess with your minds for a minute." He took in another tremendous breath and went back to work on the drum kit.

But now, his playing was very different than it had been only a few minutes earlier. It was no longer the drum solo that I remembered. Now, L.B.'s drumming was impos-ing and powerful, verging on violent. He was also playing faster than I had ever seen anyone play. And unbelievably, as he continued playing, he was picking up speed. L.B. was hitting the drums so fast and hard that he was little more than a blur. Watching him play was like to trying to watch a spinning airplane propeller or a hummingbird in flight. He was moving so fast that all I could see was a whirlwind of motion. It was unlike anything I had ever seen, and I was starting to get concerned. And so was almost everyone else in the room.

It was obvious that Jon didn't have a clue as to what was going on, but the rest of us were shooting each other ner-vous glances. The boom of the drums was deafening, and

L.B. was cycling through the kit faster and faster with each swing of the stick. Faster and faster, over and over again. L.B. was moving too fast for human eyes and minds to process. Now I was far beyond concerned. I was terrified. I was convinced that it was impossible for a human to move so fast, and I remember thinking that if it went on much longer, L.B. would injure himself or maybe even die.

Just as I was about to jump up from the couch and put an end to it, a crackling sound even louder than the boom of the drums reverberated throughout the basement. I felt the sting of an electrical charge dancing across my skin. I turned my head and looked across the room at Trice. He was still sitting at the end of the couch. In the doorway next to him I could see slowly rotating shafts of shadow. It was the exact same thing I had seen on the landing at the top of the stairs the day Chuck and I had discovered the map.

A portal was opening in the doorway. A blinding flash of blue light burst from the portal, and the entire room started to flux and flicker like an old black-and-white film. A swarm of spinning shadows engulfed the ceiling and the walls in the basement. It was like a flock of unseen birds was circling the room and projecting their silhouettes onto the walls.

I saw a second flash of blue light, and the portal disappeared. Standing in the doorway where the portal had been was the gray man. Before I could think or even move, I was overcome with extreme vertigo. The room in front of me tilted and levitated like it had been ripped from the reality of the world. It came spinning toward me with blinding speed. The vision was so chaotic that I could no longer see clearly.

Over the sound of the drums I could hear Jon screaming. I felt Chuck's hand grasp my arm and the crisp sting of his fingers digging into my flesh. The pain focused my mind, and my vision began to clear. I looked at Chuck. His face was ghostly white, and tears were streaming from his red eyes. He was backed as tightly as possible against the corner of the wall.

I turned and looked across the room. Trice and Jeff were still on the couch. They were also backed tightly against the wall. Jon was sitting between them and was still screaming. Everyone was staring in disbelief at the center of the room. I turned my head and looked at L.B. He was still behind the drum kit, still a blur of speed and motion. Standing beside him was the gray man. The swarm of shadows engulfed the ceiling and the walls as the gray man rose two feet into the air and hovered there. The faceless apparition extended his hand over L.B.'s head and spread his fingers. The gesture was reminiscent of a puppeteer working the crossbar of a marionette.

The gray man rose even higher into the air and clenched his hand into a fist. A stage light hanging in the far corner of the room came flying off the wall and hurtling across the room. It went crashing into the drums and fell in pieces to the floor. L.B. let out a horrific scream, and his drumsticks came flying out of his hands. He grabbed at his chest and curled up into a ball. He fell off the throne and landed on the floor behind his drum set screaming, "Oh my God, oh my God, oh my God, oh my God," over and over again.

A ring of fire appeared on the floor below the gray man's feet. But this time it wasn't blue. This time the ring of fire was black. The room filled with the sound of crackling static electricity. There was a loud whoosh as the gray man was sucked down into the ring of fire and vanished into nothingness. The basement stunk of decay and smoldering ashes.

Chuck and I jumped off the couch and rushed to L.B.'s side. He couldn't stand, but we helped him to sit up on the floor. With tears streaming from his eyes, he looked up at us and said, "All I could hear was the voice of my drum teacher from high school. It was like a tape of his voice was playing inside my head, repeating over and over again, faster and faster: 1 2 3 4, 1 2 3 4, 1 2 3 4, 1 2 3 4." Trice jumped up off the couch. He just stood there staring wide-eyed at the watch strapped to his wrist. He tapped the glass face of the watch with his fingertip and exclaimed, "1 2 3 4!" It was exactly 12:34 AM.

As Chuck and I were still kneeling on the floor attending to L.B., I told Trice to get Jon upstairs and out of the basement. Jon didn't need to see anything more than he already had. As Trice was leading Jon from the room, Angie walked into the basement. Her face was pale, and she looked fatigued. A blanket was draped over her shoulders, and she was shivering. She'd had a paranormal experience of her own and had an amazing tale to tell.

Angie told us that even though she had never gotten out of the easy chair in the living room, she had seen and heard everything that had transpired in the basement. She told us that as she was sitting and watching TV, she was overcome by a strange feeling and thought she might be getting ill. She had suddenly become very cold and felt sick to her stomach.

Angie told us that she was just about to go to the basement to look for Chuck when she felt a part of herself drifting up and out of her body. She described the sensation as being very similar to flying. If I had known then what know now, I would have equated what Angie experienced to astral travel, but at the time not a single one of us possessed any experience or understanding of metaphysics.

Angie's consciousness had left her body and then floated through the kitchen and down the stairs to the basement. While her physical self was sitting in the easy chair in the living room, she had seen and heard everything that had happened downstairs. She was able to describe in exact detail what the rest of us had seen and heard.

But unlike the rest of us, Angie believed that the entire thing had been a hallucination. She believed that she had gotten ill to the point of seeing and hearing things that weren't really happening. Angie added that she had also considered the possibility that she might even be losing her mind. And despite knowledge to the contrary, Chuck immediately backed up those notions. After everything that we'd been through, Chuck was still shielding Angie from the truth. But Angie was Chuck's woman, and it wasn't my business to interfere with their relationship. For the moment, I had more important things to see to.

As Chuck led Angie upstairs to get some rest, Jeff and I helped L.B. to his feet. Trice was upstairs in the living room trying to help Jon calm down. L.B. was still terribly shaken up, but other than that, he appeared to be uninjured. He mind was foggy, and his memories of the incident were vague at best. He hadn't seen the gray man materialize in the room or even been aware of his presence. All he remembered was the sound of his former drum teacher's voice inside his mind and the feeling of losing control over his own body.

What we had all just seen and experienced had serious implications. But for the time being, we couldn't discuss it openly. We knew that we couldn't tell Jon the truth about what had happened, so I came up with something off the cuff. I walked upstairs to the living room and told Jon that my house was very old and haunted by the ghost of a dead relative. I explained that the ghost was what he had seen.

As it turned out, Jon was a pretty smart kid, and I could tell that he wasn't buying my bullshit. It was obvious that he knew I wasn't telling him the whole story. But I stuck to my version of the events and eventually soothed Jon's doubts. Jon was a nice enough young man, but I had met him only a few hours earlier. I didn't allow the fabrications I had told him to get under my skin. I had no intention of telling someone I barely knew about the gray man and The Force.

The events of the evening had been traumatic to say the least. I felt that it was in everyone's best interest to stay together, so I invited L.B. and the rest of my bandmates to spend the night at my house. Angie was already asleep in the guest room anyway, so the guys thanked me for the offer and agreed to stay.

Jon sheepishly asked me if he could also stay the night at my house. He told me that his parents were out of town for the weekend and that he didn't want to sleep in his house all by himself. After what Jon had been through, I didn't blame him one bit for not wanting to be alone. I'd been in that same situation myself and knew firsthand how unpleasant it was.

I told Jon that he was more than welcome to stay and that he could sleep in my bedroom. Jon said that he didn't want to be an inconvenience and would be more than happy to crash on the floor or the couch. "Anywhere but in the basement," he added. I told Jon that I seriously doubted that I would get any sleep tonight and that he should just accept the offer to sleep in my bed. But there was more to my offer than just being a good host. I had an agenda behind offering Jon my bed. I wanted him far enough away from the rest of us that he couldn't overhear us talking.

Thirty minutes later, Jon was asleep in my bedroom and Chuck was sleeping with Angie in the guest room upstairs. L.B. was on the couch drifting in and out of sleep, and as usual Jeff was sprawled out on the living room floor under a blanket. Trice and I were sitting at my kitchen table talking. I was pretty sure that this latest incident would push Trice over the edge, and I wasn't wrong.

After seeing the gray man for the first time with his own eyes, Trice was absolutely convinced that we were dealing with a demonic entity. He stubbornly held on to this belief and was no longer willing to accept any other conclusion. More than anything else, I had come to view the gray man as a teacher and a guide, but now I wasn't so sure. Even though I still didn't believe that the gray man was something evil, this latest incident had been undeniably intense, and I found myself questioning whether or not we had any control whatsoever over The Force.

During the trip to Arvada, L.B. had acted like a spoiled little child and had been spanked for it. For reasons of vanity and his own self-interest, L.B. had disregarded his commitment to remain silent about The Force. He had shown others his darker side, and doing so had come with a price. Judgment had been passed, and the sentence had been executed. In my opinion, it was as simple as that.

But the bottom line was that the gray man had punished L.B. for his indiscretions. He had taken control of L.B.'s body and mind, and such an extreme display of power carried staggering implications. Had aligning ourselves with The Force really been the blessing it had appeared to be? Or had it placed us squarely under the boot of a relentless taskmaster? I couldn't help but wonder how far the gray man would be willing to go to punish us if we screwed up in the future. Would he physically hurt us? Or even worse than hurt us? I didn't know, and not knowing planted a seed of doubt in my mind.

I found myself questioning everything I had believed in for the last two years of my life. I felt all sense of power slipping through my fingers. Were we really in control of our own destinies? As the gray man was hovering in the air, I had seen something that no one else in the room had seen. In that moment, I had seen time reset exactly three times. Each time it had reset, the gray man had projected a vision into my mind. The visions were familiar to me. They were visions from the dream I'd had over and over again many months earlier. They were visions from the parts of the dream I couldn't remember. But now, every facet of the dream was defined, every face intact.

As time reset, I was shown a vision of how Entropy had been just a month earlier. We were young and happy, full of promise and magic. We were an invincible force hungry for success.

Time reset again, and I was shown a vision of Entropy five years in the future. In this vision, we had sailed overseas and were performing for a massive audience inside an open-roofed stadium. In this vision, we were famous musicians.

I saw time reset a third and final time, and I was shown a vision of Entropy that was profoundly disturbing. In this vision, we had allowed our own fears to destroy us. I saw us as old men, alone and separated from each other by our own obstinacies and many years of time. One of us was dead and buried in the ground.

The gray man had shown me a vision of the recent past and two very different possible futures. As I sat at the kitchen table looking at Trice, I pondered what that future might be. I couldn't help but feel that we'd already chosen that future for ourselves.

The Visit

It was a dismal and rainy morning in Fort Collins the day after the incident in the basement, and the weather was a perfect match for the mood inside my home. Despite being up so late, Chuck and Angie awoke early and started gathering their belongings. Trice and I had stayed up all night talking in the kitchen and were still sitting at the table drinking coffee. On his way out the door, Chuck poked his head inside the kitchen and informed us that he needed to drive Angie home but that he would be back directly after doing so. He knew that the band had things to discuss that we had been unable to talk about the night before.

About ten minutes after Chuck and Angie left, Jeff and L.B. came stumbling into the kitchen in search of coffee and Jon emerged from my bedroom. I told Jon that he was more than welcome to share in the coffee and a bite of breakfast, but he quickly declined my offer. He thanked me for the use of my bedroom and said his goodbyes. The sun was finally up, and it was obvious that Jon had spent all the time in my home that he cared to.

Thirty minutes after Jeff and L.B. drained their second pot of coffee and raided my fridge, Chuck pulled back into the driveway and came inside. The five of us made our way to the living room to sit down together and discuss what had happened the night before.

L.B. had experienced something completely different than the rest of us had, and I was eager to hear his side of the story. Even though L.B. hadn't seen the apparition or the other bizarre goings-on with his own eyes, for obvious reasons the incident had affected him the most negatively. The impression I had gotten was that the gray man had been controlling L.B. similar to the way a puppeteer controls a marionette, and what L.B. had to tell us only reinforced this notion.

L.B. explained that during the incident in the basement, he had no control whatsoever over his own body or mind. He told us that during the incident he had been unaware of his surroundings and that the sensation had been very similar to what he imagined being restrained and incarcerated in a prison cell would be like. Even though L.B. had done everything within his power to free himself from the constraints the gray man had placed upon him, all his efforts had been useless.

I asked L.B. if at any time during the incident he had felt like he was in physical danger. Even though L.B. tried his best to respond to my question, he couldn't give me a straight answer. It was obvious that he himself didn't know for sure whether or not the gray man had been intent on doing him harm. But danger aside, the one thing L.B. knew for sure was that he never wanted to experience anything like the incident ever again. The event had been extremely traumatizing, and L.B. told us that he was afraid to go anywhere near the basement or even his own drum set. He told us that he had no idea when he would feel up to playing again.

Trice was the next to speak, and before he even opened his mouth, I knew what he was going to say. To the best of my knowledge, Trice had never mentioned anything about demonic forces to the other guys, and I was more than a little interested in seeing how they would react to his statements. As it turned out, the guys reacted pretty much like I figured they would. I had been close friends with all of my bandmates for a long time now, and I knew their personalities inside and out. I didn't need clairvoyance to know how they would respond.

Just as I knew he would, Trice started out by saying that he believed the members of Entropy were under the influence of an evil entity. He told us that he believed the gray man was a demon, perhaps even Satan himself. Trice went on and on about demonic forces and entities for well over thirty minutes. He concluded his monologue by saying that, in his opinion, aligning ourselves with the gray man had secured each and every one of us a place in hell. After Trice finished speaking I leaned back in my chair and awaited my bandmates' inevitable reactions.

After hearing Trice speak, L.B. took his words to heart and broke down in tears. Our drummer was the youngest member of the band, and I knew that out of the five of us his character traits made him the most susceptible to persuasion. Even though L.B. had no memories of the gray man materializing in the basement, his mind and body had been taken over by an otherworldly power. He was leaning heavily in favor of Trice's way of thinking.

Chuck was the next person to express his opinion, and what he had to say took me by surprise. Chuck was beyond pissed. He viewed what the gray man had done to L.B. as nothing short of a personal attack. Chuck had known L.B. longer than the rest of us and was responsible for bringing him into the band. He had taken L.B. under his wing and was devoted to keeping him safe. Chuck wanted vengeance for the punishment that had been exacted on our drummer. From the beginning, Chuck had been the most vocal advocate of the gray man, but now his attitude had shifted dramatically. He believed that our alliance with the gray man had turned sour and that we needed to put an end to it.

After Chuck finished speaking, I told my bandmates that even though I had no idea exactly who or what the gray man really was, I was intent on exploring things further. I told them that I believed the true potential of the gray man and The Force had yet to be tapped and that Entropy's best prospects for the future still lay in his hands. Right or wrong, after everything I had seen and experienced, I was unwilling to let go of the power of The Force without a fight.

But as desperately as I wanted to hang on to what we had, the sad truth was that the members of Entropy were now very much at odds with each other, and I could feel the power of the seven draining away. But amidst the infighting, there was one more member of Entropy to be heard from. When we finally got around to asking Jeff what his opinion was, he simply stated, "You're all full of shit." And out of all of our opinions, Jeff's was without a doubt the most accurate.

Jeff's point was that we were dealing with otherworldly forces and that none of us had a clue what those forces really were. He pointed out that we were speaking in absolutes about the supernatural and that none of us was qualified to do so. Jeff thought we were all acting like a bunch of fools. And he wasn't wrong. As the debate went on, the five of us started pointing fingers and getting in each other's faces. We were talking over each other and getting louder and louder by the second. The conversation was getting frenzied, and I was certain that if it went on for much longer, we would all walk away with hard feelings. Maybe even something worse than hard feelings. Just as I was about to tell the guys that enough was enough and that we needed to shelve the debate for another day, over the din of our voices I heard the sound of someone knocking on my front door.

Upon hearing the sound of knocking, I told the rest of the guys to chill out and sit down. As Chuck sat back down on the couch he quipped, "The last fucking thing we need right now is a visitor." Even though I couldn't argue with Chuck's statement, on my way to answer the door I came to the conclusion that an interruption might just be a good thing. At the very least, it would provide a break in the action and give the five of us an opportunity to cool down.

As I turned the knob and opened the door, I saw that a young black man wearing polyester slacks and a gray V-neck sweater was standing on my front porch. I instantly assumed he was a salesman. The man appeared to be in his late twenties and was without a doubt one of the most striking young men I had ever seen. In a word, he was beautiful. The man had short, curly black hair and a perfectly trimmed goatee. He was slight of stature, even smaller than Trice, and something about him just glowed. If pressed to describe the man's appearance, I would have said he was a cross between an angel and an imp. I had never laid eyes on the man before, and yet somehow I had the impression that I had known him for a very long time.

I unlatched the screen door, and the black man looked up at me and smiled. He extended his hand, and in a voice that matched his face perfectly he said, "I've heard about Entropy and I'm here to offer you my help." I was inexplicably drawn to the man, and after sharing a handshake I invited him to come inside. Standing in the foyer, the man waved at the rest of the guys and gave them an irresistible smile. The man introduced himself as Gabriel Manning, but quickly added that "everyone just calls me Gabe."

I invited Gabe to have a seat in the living room. Without hesitation, he walked over and sat down on the couch directly between Chuck and L.B. My bandmates all looked Gabe over curiously. It was clear that they were interested in who this man might be. After personally introducing himself to each of the guys and shaking their hands, Gabe dispensed with any further pleasantries and went straight to the topic of Entropy.

Just as Gabe had told me at the front door, he explained to the rest of the guys that he was here to help the band. Gabe told us that he wasn't a promoter or an entertainment agent, but just a straightforward man who was interested in Entropy and our music. He told us that he had helped other bands attain their dreams of success over the years and that he was confident he could help Entropy realize that very same dream. Gabe told us that he could put us in touch with some very important people in the music industry, not the least of whom was a well-known producer for a major record label.

Gabe went on to tell us that he possessed a certain degree of influence and that if we were willing to follow his lead, Entropy could be famous in less than two years' time. After the tragic events in Arvada, this was exciting news. We had seen our chance for success slip away, and we had been powerless to stop it. But once again, the chance for success appeared to be within our grasp. The band had spent the last month wading through our own shit with seemingly no way out, and we were all interested in hearing exactly how Gabe intended to help us. But Chuck in particular was more than just interested. His brow was furrowed and he was looking at Gabe cautiously. Chuck shifted uncomfortably on the couch. He looked Gabe directly in the eyes and asked, "Do I know you? Have we met before?"

Gabe's smiled at Chuck. He shook his head and said, "No, I don't think so."

Gabe wasn't the kind of man that a person easily forgets, and Chuck genuinely seemed to recognize him. It was obvious that something had Chuck on edge, and I could feel the tension building in the room.

As if in an effort to break that tension, Gabe looked at Chuck and said, "So I hear you have an Ibanez Iceman from the seventies, is that right?"

Chuck nodded and said, "Yes, that's right."

"Is it the original guitar?" Gabe continued. "The one your father bought you just before he died?"

Chuck's entire body jerked violently. It looked like an involuntary reaction. I didn't have a clue as to why he was acting so strangely. But what the rest of us didn't know at the time was that Chuck's father had bought him the Iceman just before he was killed in action and that Chuck was the only living person who knew that. He had never told anyone about the guitar's true origins. Not us, not Angie, no one. But somehow Gabe knew.

Chuck took in a deep breath. He leaned in close to Gabe and said, "I'm going to ask you one more time, and I want a straight answer. Do I know you?"

Gabe didn't say a word. He just sat there smiling. Without forewarning, Chuck suddenly jumped up from the couch. He had jumped up so quickly that it startled everyone in the room. Chuck just stood there looking down at Gabe with an intense stare. It was like Chuck was seeing beyond the façade of flesh, seeing deep inside of Gabe. What was he seeing that the rest of us weren't? Chuck's eyes suddenly grew wide. The look on his face was the look of a man who had just had an epiphany. Chuck frantically pointed his finger at Gabe and exclaimed, "It's him!" He looked around the room at the rest of us and repeated, "It's him!"

I got up out of my chair and looked at Gabe. I didn't understand what Chuck was talking about. I looked at the rest of my bandmates. They were every bit as confused as I was. I looked back at Chuck and saw that his face was now filled with rage. Chuck reached down, grabbed Gabe by the arms, and pulled him up and off the couch. "Tell me your real name," Chuck demanded. "Tell me your real fucking name!"

Gabe just stood there smiling. I tried without success to comprehend what was happening. I looked around the room and saw that my bandmates were also wide-eyed and staring at Gabe. At that moment, everything came together in my mind like the answer to a riddle. I now understood. Chuck believed that Gabe was the embodiment of the entity. He believed that Gabe was the gray man made flesh and blood.

Chuck grabbed Gabe by both arms and started shaking him violently. "What did you do to us?" Chuck screamed. "What did you do to my friend?"

The scene playing out in front of me was like something from a nightmare. Everything seemed surreal. Chuck was out of control, and it was obvious that he was intent on doing Gabe harm. And unbelievably, Trice and L.B. were spurring him on. I was about to cry out for Chuck to stop what he was doing, but before I could get the words out of my mouth, Jeff went rushing over and pushed Chuck away from Gabe. As Jeff held Chuck back, he looked at me and shouted, "Get him out of here now! Get him out before he gets hurt!"

I hurried over to Gabe and took him gently by the arm. I led him to the foyer and opened the front door. The sight behind me in the living room was pure chaos. Jeff was struggling to hold back Chuck, and my bandmates were all screaming at each other. Gabe and I stepped onto the front porch, and I quickly closed the door behind me.

It was still drab and rainy outside, and as I stood there on the porch with Gabe, my spirit felt as dreary as the weather. I was only twenty-two years old, but I felt ancient and thin, like a person who had experienced too much hardship in his lifetime. The world around me was colorless and two-dimensional. I no longer knew what to think or believe. *Could my bandmates be right?* I wondered. *Could Gabe really be the gray man? Or was he just a man?*

I searched Gabe's eyes for an answer. I found nothing. Still smiling, Gabe just stood there on the porch looking back at me. I wanted to ask him who he really was, but I didn't. I knew that no matter what the truth was, Gabe would tell me that he was just a man. Not knowing what else to do or say, I apologized to Gabe for what had happened and told him that it would probably be best if he just went on his way.

Gabe extended his hand to me for a second time, and I took it. It was warm and comforting, like the hand of a beloved grandfather. Gabe reached into his pants pocket. He pulled out a small, folded piece of paper and placed it in my hand. He stepped down off the porch and strolled to the sidewalk. I wanted to call out to Gabe and ask him if there was still hope for us, but I didn't. I just stood there in silence and watched him walk away until he disappeared from view.

Stepping back inside the house, I saw that things were no better than they had been before I went outside with Gabe. In fact, the situation was much worse. Chuck and Jeff were still at each other's throats and on the verge of coming to blows. L.B. was huddled on the couch with tears in his eyes, and Trice was sitting next to him ranting about the Devil. My bandmates were all acting as though they had lost their minds. And for my part, "lost" was as good a word as any to describe me. I had lost all sense of reality, all sense of control. I knew that if we had any chance of keeping Entropy together, we had to talk things out here and now. I'd had my fill of turmoil, and I demanded that everyone shut up and sit the fuck down. My words weren't well received.

Chuck and Jeff were still enraged with one another and unwilling to listen to reason. Chuck instructed L.B. to gather his things and told me that I could go screw myself. Two minutes later, they were headed out the front door.

Jeff told me that he needed to cool down and left directly behind L.B. and Chuck. I knew that Jeff would be willing to talk things through, but this clearly wasn't the time or place. I decided it was best to just let him go on his way.

After the others had gone, I tried to reach out to Trice, but he was still so frantic that it was impossible to have a rational conversation with him. He was still babbling on about demons and dark forces. Trice even went so far as to say that as long as the gray man was a part of Entropy, he would never sign a recording contract. He equated it to signing his name in blood on a contract with the Devil. Upon hearing this come out of Trice's mouth, I'd finally had enough of his bullshit. I got right up in his face and shouted, "You need help, Trice. You need help bad!"

Trice gave me a look that was somewhere between anger and despair. He got up from where he was sitting on the couch and walked across the room to the desk to get his car keys. As Trice grabbed his keys, the telephone sitting on the desk started ringing. Trice stared down at the phone. I really didn't expect him to answer it, but he did. He picked up the receiver on the third ring and held it to his ear. Trice's eyes narrowed as he listened to the voice on the other end of the line. A moment later, all of the life drained out of his face. The receiver slipped from his hand and went crashing down on top of the desk. Trice hurried over to the front door. He quickly opened it, stepped across the threshold, and slammed the door shut behind him. The sound was hollow as it echoed throughout my empty house.

The Arrow of Time

I was twenty-two years old on the day that Entropy claimed itself. And I was fifty-two years old on the day I sat down at the desk in my living room and started writing our story. Thirty years have passed since the time of Entropy and the gray man, thirty years since I've felt the power of seven and the presence of The Force. But the truth is that even after all this time, the gray man has never really left us. At least not completely. And all the things we experienced in that long ago time still affect our lives to this very day.

To no one's surprise, Trice became a very religious man after Entropy disbanded. He continued his musical career by dedicating his adult life to being the band director for his church. Out of the five members of Entropy, the gray man had affected Trice the most negatively. He was terrified of that otherworldly power and sought solace in his convictions.

To this day, Trice believes that if Entropy had become a major success, we would have witnessed extreme supernatural events taking place at our concerts. He believes that during our concerts, we would have witnessed ghostly apparitions, members of the audience speaking in tongues, and spontaneous acts of healing. But he also believes that these supernatural events would not have been the acts of a kind and loving God, but acts of evil cleverly disguised to lure our unsuspecting fans into an alliance with the forces of darkness. He believes that Entropy would have ended up being Satan's messengers and puppets.

Trice and I have remained lifelong friends, but somewhere over the distance of time we lost the closeness we once shared. And in case you've been wondering what Trice heard over the telephone on the day that Entropy died, I should probably tell you. I didn't know myself for the longest time, but Trice eventually confided in me. As I'm sure you recall, right before the telephone rang and Trice answered it, I told him the following: "You need help, Trice. You need help bad!" When Trice answered the telephone that day, the voice on the other end of the line had told him, "You need help, Trice. You need help bad!" The voice on the telephone was dark and brimming with rage. Trice had heard that exact same voice telling him the exact same thing almost two years earlier on the morning he had answered the telephone after the unplugged alarm clock had turned on by itself on the staircase.

You may also be wondering what became of our friend Tom Willson. As you may recall, many years earlier Tom had been diagnosed with terminal cancer and had been told by his doctors that he had only a few months to live. You may also recall that during Entropy's concert in Colorado Springs, a young black man had raised Tom's spirits. After Entropy disbanded, Tom more or less became a hermit, and he isolated himself from his friends and family. I wondered for a long time if Tom had died from his cancer and whether the young man who had comforted him at the concert had been Gabriel Manning.

Approximately ten years after the time of Entropy, I received a phone call from Tom. During our conversation I learned that even though Tom still carried the disease and couldn't afford to pay for treatment, he had miraculously bucked the odds and had managed to live many years beyond what his doctors had predicted. Based on Tom's description, I also learned that the young black man who had raised his spirits at the concert was an exact physical match for Gabriel. Less than a year after Tom called me, he finally succumbed to the cancer and passed away. There is no doubt in my mind that the man who had given Tom comfort at the concert was none other than Gabriel Manning.

Chuck also found peace in religion, although I've been told that he was never as devout as Trice. The last time I saw Chuck, his jet-black hair had grayed and he was covered in tattoos. I was delighted to discover that after all these years, he still had the Ibanez Iceman his father had gifted him with before he died. After the time of Entropy, Chuck and I also remained close, but as is all too often the case, we eventually lost track of each other.

But seven years after Entropy disbanded, Chuck telephoned me with some alarming news. He told me that earlier in the day he had been showering, and that as he was standing in front of the tub drying off, through the bathroom doorway he had seen the gray man materialize in his bedroom. Chuck told me that although the materialization had been brief, he got the distinct impression that the gray man wanted to hurt me, perhaps even kill me.

Chuck was very serious about what he was telling me. I could hear it in his voice. Chuck told me that he was very concerned about my well-being and made me promise to watch my back. As I hung up the phone, my hands were trembling. My wife and I were expecting our first child, and I was terrified by the implications of the gray man wanting to do me harm. If an otherworldly entity as powerful as the gray man wanted to hurt me, there was absolutely nothing I could do to prevent it from happening. I spent the next three weeks in a constant state of anxiety. But as the days went by without incident, I started to relax and my fears eventually became nothing more than a distant memory. To my knowledge, the gray man has never visited Chuck again.

As for L.B., I've only seen him once in the last thirty years and that was shortly after Entropy had disbanded. What I know about his current life and whereabouts I recently learned from Trice. I was thrilled to hear that L.B. is alive and well and living in Indiana. I was also pleased to hear that, unlike the rest of us, L.B. has made a lifelong career out of music.

According to Trice, L.B. has taught percussion at many schools across the country and has served as the marching band director for a major university. He has won numerous awards for his musical compositions and is endorsed by a major drum manufacturer. He has also recorded numerous commercials and albums as a studio drummer. From the sound of things, L.B. has made a good life for himself with his music, and I expected nothing less from someone with his diverse talents. I recently spent several weeks trying to track down L.B. without success. It is unknown whether or not he has had any contact with the gray man over the last thirty years or how much he remembers about his days with Entropy.

Jeff was the most tenacious of all my former bandmates, and he did a good job of staying in contact with all of us. The two years that Entropy spent together was a very special time in Jeff's life, and he refused to allow his memories of those days to lose their shine. He would often visit me at my home to talk about the band and everything we experienced. But as time went on, Jeff became more and more at odds with life. In his later years, Jeff suffered from physical and mental ailments that made it impossible for him to lead a normal existence. He eventually became addicted to hard drugs, and his addictions killed him. Jeff was laid to rest in a small cemetery in west Texas very close to where his mother still lives to this day.

And as for me, I've lived in the presence of the gray man my entire adult life, and I doubt that's going to change anytime soon. What I experienced with Entropy sent me on a lifelong quest to explore the boundaries of the supernatural, and after decades of research and practice, I eventually became a veteran of all things esoteric and extraordinary. Because of the gray man, I began studying metaphysics and investigating the paranormal. I have spent many years of my life searching our world for ghosts and evidence of life after death.

Because of Entropy and the gray man, I became a writer and have lived a life filled with astonishment and magic. I'm the person I am today because of the gray man, and I believe that somewhere along the line, he and I became synonymous. I believe that on the day that Chuck and I followed the map to the top of the stairs and I saw into the portal, something incredible happened. I believe that in that moment, a part of the gray man transferred into me and that a part of myself possibly transferred into him. I believe that in that moment, we became an inseparable part of each other.

The days I spent with Entropy were so alive that it's difficult for me to look back on them now without viewing them as living, breathing things. Trying to keep Entropy together was like trying to capture lightning in a bottle. We became so entangled in the supernatural that in many ways during our time together, we lived a separate existence from everyone else on the planet. In reflection, it would have been impossible to keep the band together and still maintain our sense of reality and coexist with the outside world. The things I experienced with Entropy were as wondrous as they were scary, and I think that's what I loved about them the most.

The gray man rarely appears to me in person anymore, but he emerges in other ways. He still speaks to me through numbers on the clock, and I can often feel his unmistakable presence inside my home. In fact, as I was writing this story, the gray man spoke to me relentlessly. As the days went by, the numeric language of his voice became my constant companion. To no surprise, I even finished writing this book on the tenth day of the tenth month of the year.

I still have my clairvoyance, but it's never gotten much stronger than it was during the time of Entropy. I can still predict minor events, though I'm not even close to being a genuine psychic. But it doesn't take a psychic to realize that The Force doesn't exist inside a rock 'n' roll band or even an entity from another world. The Force is a way of experiencing a superlative life. It's that rare flash of brilliance. It's a perfect and elusive moment in time, not a physical object that can be put on display for the entire world to see.

The Force is something that can be experienced but never truly owned. Yes, the gray man and The Force have been an integral part of my life for over thirty years now, and there is undoubtedly much more to the story of Entropy than I can remember. I'm certain that there are parts of our story that are beyond my recollection and that those lost memories are still adrift somewhere in the vagaries of time.

I have told you our story as I lived it and remember it, and for now at least that's good enough for me. But as a storyteller, a single question still haunts me: How do you finish telling a story that has never really ended? Upon reflection, I realize that our present-day stories aren't what really matter. This is the story of Entropy, and that story ended thirty years ago. And thirty years ago, I was sitting at the desk in my living room thinking about my life and trying to figure out how everything had gone so wrong...

After my bandmates walked out the door that day, I spent the better part of an hour sitting alone at the desk in my living room. I sat there thinking about the last two years of my life and everything I had seen and done. I thought about Entropy and everything we had experienced together. I thought about the gray man, and I wondered if I would ever see him again.

It would have been easy enough for me to blame Entropy's downfall on L.B.'s actions in Arvada, but the truth was that my own transgressions were to blame. We had shown our darker sides, and clearly each and every one of us had failed. But my failure was by far the most egregious. I was the bandleader, the captain of the ship. It was my job to steer that ship through the stormy seas and keep my crew safe and intact. I had botched that job terribly. And as desperately as I wanted to right the ship and sail her to calmer waters, I knew that it was too late.

I slid open the desk drawer in front of me and pulled out the folded piece of paper that Gabriel had given me on the front porch. I unfolded the paper and looked at it for the third time. Written on the paper were a name and telephone number. I didn't recognize the number, but I certainly did the name. The name belonged to a producer who worked for a very well-known record label. Being given such a name and number was everything I'd desired for many years. And now I was holding it in my hand. I should have been exhilarated, on top of the world. But I wasn't. No matter how much I wanted to believe otherwise, Entropy was dead. The only thing left to do was chisel the date on the headstone.

I telephoned Chuck and told him I was leaving the band. By then Chuck had calmed down considerably, and he told me he understood. He told me there probably wasn't a band left to leave, anyway. I hung up the phone and walked to my bedroom with the piece of paper in my hand. I opened the top drawer of my dresser and placed the paper on top of the poem that had been given to me by the gray man. I slid the drawer closed and sat down on the end of my bed. The room was silent and still.

As I sat there in my bedroom, I thought about the time I had spent on the front porch with Gabe. I found myself wishing that I could revisit that moment. I wished that I had done things differently. I thought about all the things I should have said and asked that I didn't. But I knew that all the wishing in the world wouldn't change things or bring Gabe back. I was profoundly saddened by that fact.

I cannot tell you with any certainty if that beautiful young man was flesh and blood. I cannot tell you with any certainty that he was something more than that. What I can tell you is that the moment Gabriel walked away and disappeared from sight, I knew I would never see him again. In that moment, I knew that The Force was gone.

To Write to the Author

If you wish to contact the author or would like more information about this book, please write to the author in care of Llewellyn Worldwide Ltd. and we will forward your request. Both the author and publisher appreciate hearing from you and learning of your enjoyment of this book and how it has helped you. Llewellyn Worldwide Ltd. cannot guarantee that every letter written to the author can be answered, but all will be forwarded. Please write to:

Marcus F. Griffin
% Llewellyn Worldwide
2143 Wooddale Drive
Woodbury, MN 55125-2989

Please enclose a self-addressed stamped envelope for reply, or $1.00 to cover costs. If outside the U.S.A., enclose an international postal reply coupon.

GET MORE AT LLEWELLYN.COM

Visit us online to browse hundreds of our books and decks, plus sign up to receive our e-newsletters and exclusive online offers.

- **Free tarot readings • Spell-a-Day • Moon phases**
- **Recipes, spells, and tips • Blogs • Encyclopedia**
- **Author interviews, articles, and upcoming events**

GET SOCIAL WITH LLEWELLYN

Find us on Facebook

www.Facebook.com/LlewellynBooks

Follow us on twitter™

www.Twitter.com/Llewellynbooks

GET BOOKS AT LLEWELLYN

LLEWELLYN ORDERING INFORMATION

Order online: Visit our website at www.llewellyn.com to select your books and place an order on our secure server.

Order by phone:
- Call toll free within the U.S. at 1-877-NEW-WRLD (1-877-639-9753)
- Call toll free within Canada at 1-866-NEW-WRLD (1-866-639-9753)
- We accept VISA, MasterCard, and American Express

Order by mail:
Send the full price of your order (MN residents add 6.875% sales tax) in U.S. funds, plus postage and handling to: Llewellyn Worldwide, 2143 Wooddale Drive Woodbury, MN 55125-2989

POSTAGE AND HANDLING

STANDARD (U.S. & Canada):
(Please allow 12 business days)
$25.00 and under, add $4.00.
$25.01 and over, FREE SHIPPING.

INTERNATIONAL ORDERS (airmail only):
$16.00 for one book, plus $3.00 for each additional book.

Visit us online for more shipping options.
Prices subject to change.

FREE CATALOG!

To order, call 1-877-NEW-WRLD ext. 8236 or visit our website

Marcus F. Griffin

Foreword by Jeff Belanger

EXTREME
PARANORMAL
INVESTIGATIONS

The Blood Farm Horror,
the Legend of Primrose Road,
and Other Disturbing Hauntings

Extreme Paranormal Investigations
The Blood Farm Horror, the Legend of Primrose Road, and Other Disturbing Hauntings
Marcus F. Griffin
Foreword by Ghostvillage.com founder and author Jeff Belanger

Set foot inside the bone-chilling, dangerous, and sometimes downright terrifying world of extreme paranormal investigations. Join Marcus F. Griffin, Wiccan priest and founder of Witches in Search of the Paranormal (WISP), as he and his team explore the Midwest's most haunted properties. These investigations include the creepiest-of-the-creepy cases WISP has tackled over the years, many of them in locations that had never before been investigated. These true-case files include investigations of Okie Pinokie and the Demon Pillar Pigs, the Ghost Children of Munchkinland Cemetery, and the Legend of Primrose Road. Readers will also get an inside glimpse of previously inaccessible places, such as the former Jeffrey Dahmer property as WISP searches for the notorious serial killer's spirit, and the farm that belonged to Belle Gunness, America's first female serial killer and the perpetrator of the Blood Farm Horror.

978-0-7387-2697-7, 264 pp., 5³⁄₁₆ x 8 $15.95

THE NIGHTMARE
ON BAXTER ROAD

ANATOMY *of a*
HAUNTING

LEE STRONG

Anatomy of a Haunting
The Nightmare on Baxter Road
LEE STRONG

This is the true story of one couple's descent into darkness. In 1981, Jon and Carlie Summers moved into an inherited home in rural Iowa, leaving behind their workaday lives as a lawyer and a professor in Chicago. Soon after moving in, Jon and Carlie's lives begin a downward spiral as Carlie experiences violent dreams, possessions, hallucinations, and physical illness. Through old journals, nightmares, and personal encounters with evil, Carlie relives the history of the house, embodying its past of abuse, denial, obsession, broken lives, and death.

Anatomy of a Haunting is a terrifying true story that leaves Jon dead and pushes Carlie to the brink of insanity. Through interviews and exhaustive research into the 150-year-old McPherson house, author Lee Strong delves into the history of the haunting and paints a nightmarish picture of one couple's descent into supernatural madness.

978-0-7387-3552-8, 360 pp. 6 x 9   **$16.99**

ADVENTURES OF A
GHOST HUNTER

MY INVESTIGATIONS INTO THE DARKNESS

ADAM NORI

Adventures of a Ghost Hunter
My Investigations into the Darkness
ADAM NORI

Some people tell ghost stories. Adam Nori is living one.

A founding member of the Minnesota Paranormal Study Group, Adam Nori began investigating ghosts at ten years old. In *Adventures of a Ghost Hunter*, Nori tells the most chilling tales of his investigations. Driven by his desire to pay tribute to a favorite uncle, Nori and his team utilize a blend of technology, research, and intuition to investigate the most haunted places in the Midwest.

Investigating haunted homes, museums, cemeteries, and even a bus station, the Minnesota Paranormal Study Group combines scientific data collection with psychic communication. Be afraid as the group channels spirits, witnesses apparitions, and captures EVPs, and be warmed as Nori develops helpful, healing relationships with his frightened clients. Nori's passion for investigating, teaching, and raising money for historical preservation is carried out with gratitude and earnestness—this is one ghost hunter you'll find yourself rooting for!

978-0-7387-3541-2, 240 pp., 5³⁄₁₆ x 8   **$14.99**

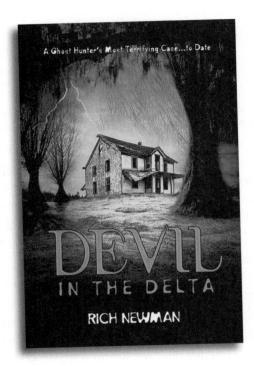

A Ghost Hunter's Most Terrifying Case...to Date

DEVIL
IN THE DELTA

RICH NEWMAN

Devil in the Delta
A Ghost Hunter's Most Terrifying Case . . . to Date
RICH NEWMAN

When author Rich Newman first arrives at the battered doublewide trailer deep in the Mississippi delta, it's clear that this is no ordinary haunting. Called from Memphis to assist a local ghost hunting team, Newman's investigation of the Martin house has become his most terrifying and mysterious case. What starts out as a malicious assault manifesting as deep rumbling sounds quickly spirals into a story of obsession, possession, witchcraft, and murder. When the evidence becomes overwhelming, long-buried memories from Newman's own past come back to haunt him—memories he'd rather forget. Collecting physical evidence, researching the violent history of the property, and sorting through the spiritual implications of demons, Newman's investigation of the Martin house is unlike any other.

978-0-7387-3516-0, 240 pp., 5³⁄₁₆ x 8   **$14.99**

BARBARA PARKS

in the presence of

spirits

a true story of ghostly visitations

In the Presence of Spirits
A True Story of Ghostly Visitations
Barbara Parks

Traumatized by vicious poltergeist attacks that lasted five years, Barbara Parks never imagined that her deep-rooted fear of ghosts would disappear. A momentous turning point occurs when, still mourning the sudden death of a beloved friend, she receives a miraculous visit from him. This joyous experience marks her first step toward healing—and opening up to spirit world.

In the Presence of Spirits chronicles Barbara's uplifting, personal journey of gradually accepting and embracing the clairvoyant gifts that allow her to see spirits. She shares dramatic and heartwarming stories of interacting with spirits who turn up everywhere: at home, on vacation, and accompanying her patients. From the departed uncle that protects Barbara's young children from grave injury to the child spirits who bring comfort to their parents, these amazing true tales are convincing reminders that our loved ones are never far away.

978-0-7387-3352-4, 240 pp., 5³⁄₁₆ x 8   **$15.99**

VIVIAN CAMPBELL
STALKED by SPIRITS
true tales of a ghost magnet

Stalked by Spirits
True Tales of a Ghost Magnet
VIVIAN CAMPBELL

Haunted since childhood, Vivian Campbell has encountered angry wraiths, mischievous child spirits, terrorizing demons, and all sorts of bizarre, unearthly beings. Vivian relives these chilling and thrilling experiences in *Stalked by Spirits*, including how she and her family suffered violent phantom attacks, received small favors from a little girl ghost, negotiated with a demanding spirit, welcomed back a dearly departed pet, tolerated ghostly attendance at holiday dinners and Girl Scout meetings, and waged hair-raising battles with an evil entity threatening their baby daughter.

Taking us inside a variety of spirit-infested, often beautiful places—a stone mansion in the Tennessee mountains, a century-old college dorm, the first apartment she shared with her new husband, and the beloved Florida home that's been in her family for generations—these true tales vividly capture an extraordinary and haunted life.

978-0-7387-2731-8, 288 pp., 5³⁄₁₆ x 8   **$15.95**

The True Ghost Story of a
Reluctant Psychic
A Haunted Life
Debra Robinson

A Haunted Life
The True Ghost Story of a Reluctant Psychic
DEBRA ROBINSON

Debra Robinson faced haunted houses, terrifying psychic encounters, shattered dreams, and a battle with evil. But nothing prepared her for the death of the two most important people in her life.

Born psychic and raised in a religious family, Debra Robinson felt conflicted all her life about using her gifts. And when, at an early age, she attracts something evil with a Ouija board, she embarks on a lengthy battle with darkness. With her career as a professional musician taking her on the road, she experiences brushes with fame and heartbreak that serve to strengthen her resolve. Struggling to come to terms with her psychic gifts, the tragic deaths of her only child and her beloved father—and their visits from the other side—finally leave her with a sense of understanding and the strength to love herself.

978-0-7387-3641-9, 288 pp., 5³⁄₁₆ x 8   **$16.99**
